POETRY ESCAPE

IMMERSED IN WORDS

First published in Great Britain in 2025 by:

🌀YoungWriters®
Est. 1991

Young Writers
Remus House
Coltsfoot Drive
Peterborough
PE2 9BF
Telephone: 01733 890066
Website: www.youngwriters.co.uk

All Rights Reserved
Book Design by Ashley Janson
© Copyright Contributors 2025
Softback ISBN 978-1-83685-530-9
Printed and bound in the UK by BookPrintingUK
Website: www.bookprintinguk.com
YB0642CZ

FOREWORD

Since 1991 our aim here at Young Writers has been to encourage creativity in children and young adults and to inspire a love of the written word. Each competition is tailored to the relevant age group, hopefully giving each student the inspiration and incentive to create their own piece of creative writing, whether it's a poem or a short story. We truly believe that seeing their work in print gives students a sense of achievement and pride.

For our latest competition Poetry Escape, we challenged secondary school students to free their creativity and break through the barriers to express their true thoughts, using poetic techniques as their tools of escape. They had several options to choose from offering either a specific theme or a writing constraint. Alternatively they could forge their own path, because there's no such thing as a dead end where imagination is concerned.

The result is an inspiring anthology full of ideas, hopes, fears and imagination, proving that creativity really does offer escape, in whatever form you need it.

We encourage young writers to express themselves and address topics that matter to them, which sometimes means exploring sensitive or difficult topics. If you have been affected by any issues raised in this book, details on where to find help can be found at: www.youngwriters.co.uk/support.

CONTENTS

Akeley Wood School, Akeley

George Parckar (12)	1
Madeline White	2
Kai Purves	5
Zohan Mohsin	6
Ines Gherib	8
Joshua MacKinnon	10
Ollie Chapman	11
Charles Stancliffe-White (16)	12
Jayden Masarira (12)	13
Isaac Kainth	14

Ark Elvin Academy, Wembley

Jayden Gomes (15)	15
Rahima Omar	16
Shinaya Robinson	19
Aleeza Chaudhery (12)	20
Sarah-Alexandra Dulgheriu (12)	23
Waleed Ibrahemi	24
Rovito Da Costa (11)	26
Mila Johnson (12)	28
Zoha Nouman-Chohan (11)	30
Angel Gracias (16)	31
Samaira Manha	32
Maryam Hussain (12)	34
Fatma Al Enazy	35
Prince Golgis Musemina (15)	36
Aicha El Gallaf-Ajiyel	37
Selven D'Silva	38

Bentley Wood High School, Stanmore

Faiza Safi (15)	39

Sara Shahood (13)	40
Mya Ali (15)	42
Jasmine Gioiosa (13)	43
Ruqaiya Mohamed Jinnah (13)	44
Alyah Ibrahim Mohamed (16)	45
Mia Pindoria (12)	46
Anniyah Sethi (14)	47

Bexhill Academy, Bexhill-On-Sea

Theo Heritage (11)	48
Jessica Wilson (12)	50
Lucia McDermott (12)	52
Zoe Ogechi Nwuju (12)	54
Ben Ashby (12)	55
Myah Wapples (11)	56
Fraya Vaillant (12)	57
Natalia Nowicka (12)	58
Chloe Lazenby (12)	59
Daisy Wright (11)	60
Antonio Peteoaca (12)	61

Birchgrove Comprehensive School, Birchgrove

Charlie Meredith (14)	62
Jasper Higgitt (13)	64

Bolton Muslim Girls' School, Bolton

Dur Zanib (15)	65
Arfa Imran (15)	66
Haram Arfan (12)	68
Tehreem Zia (11)	70
Ayesha Faisal (11)	71

Aisha Ahmed (13)	72
Anika Mehjaben (14)	73
Afiyah Pathan (11)	74
Damil Arfan (14)	75

Caldicot School, Caldicot

Reese Lane-Mudie (13)	76
Jessica Hobbs (8)	79
Eli Bruce (13)	80
Lexi Connolly (12)	82
Ffion Davies	84
Rhian Reeks (15)	86
Emily Luke (13)	87
Nye Thomas (16)	88
Elliott Bevan (9)	90
Jess Bartlett (13)	91
Kaitlyn Williams (13)	92
Maddie Williams (13)	93
Ania Heales (13)	94
Maryam Rishi (13)	95
Talia Brigden (13)	96
Callie Sedlen (9)	97

Carrickfergus Grammar School, Carrickfergus

Kai Bennett (16)	98
Niamh McKinney (16)	100
Matthew Clarke (15)	101

Copley Academy, Stalybridge

Zulekha Farzand Ali (11)	102
Nevaeh Norton (11)	103
Nell Swettenham (12)	104
Archie Curtis-Bailey (14)	105
Saanvi Deshbhratar (13)	106
Lily Murphy (12)	107
Keane Ashton (14)	108
Darcy Gooch (11)	109
Imogen McBurnie (14)	110
Jess Clegg (13)	111
Max Van Massey (12)	112

Jan Judzewicz (11)	113
Toby McLaren (12)	114
Freya Neville-Cooper (13)	115
Phoebie Ryan (11)	116
Jessica Vickers (11)	117
Raja Akram (12)	118
Charlotte Leeming (12)	119
Elsie Foley-Turner (12)	120
Isabella Lockwood (14)	121
Lewis Blenkinsop (13)	122

Dedworth Middle School, Windsor

Deona Jaison (13)	123
Callum O'Connor (12)	124
Kaycee Ireland (13)	126
Grace Phipps (11)	127
Adan Maki (11)	128
Ruby Lock (13)	130
Dylan Turner (12)	131
Dexter Bull (12)	132
Harley Brant (12)	133
Zoha Chaudhary (12)	134
Gunn Walia (12)	135
Lucy Martin (11)	136
Roxi Hasley (12)	137
Govind Singh Sehra (12)	138
Jessica Clark (11)	139
Amber Agacy (11)	140
Desiree Lawson (12)	141
Rron Mulolli (12)	142

Denstone College, Denstone

Cameron Birchill (16)	143
William Kelly (13)	144
Izzy Houghton (12)	145
Felicity Baker (12)	146
Aidan Jones (12)	148
Bear Yates (14)	149

Devonport High School For Girls, Peverell

Isla Soper (14)	150

Gowerton School, Gowerton

Naomi Benjamin (11)	151

Kingsbury High School, Kingsbury

Pedro Goncalves Gurgel Filho (14)	152

Langley Park School For Girls, Beckenham

Issie Williams (13)	153

Sheringham High School, Sheringham

Florence Sanders (11)	155
Evie Furze (11)	156
Brieanna Baldwin (12)	157
Mabel-Faith Smith	158
Ava Mai Mardell (12)	159
Nicole Boswell (12)	160
Hannah Bennett (12)	161
Reuban Bellingham (13)	162
Jack Farmer Stowe (13)	163

The Fountain School, Bradford

Zainab Afsar (15)	164
Munibah Khan (14)	166
Mahroosh Kashif (14)	167
Ieza Mohammad (15)	168
Ramlah Said	169
Sumayyah Waqas	170
Ilsa Khan (15)	171
Juwayriyah Bint-Abbas (15)	172
Hafsa	173
Ifra Dastagir (14)	174
Naima Khan	175

Woldgate School & Sixth Form College, Pocklington

Oscar Pullen (12)	176
Jongpatana Saiyut (12)	177
Olivia Swattridge (11)	178
Fergus Wilson (12)	179
Faye Cotton (12)	180
Olivia Beck (11)	181
Gene Chandler (12)	182

Woodbridge Park Education Services, Feltham

Ruby Gardner (14)	183
Abbie Napper (15)	184

THE POEMS

To Fall, And To Rise

Falling. Falling. Falling.
Seemingly no way to turn around, yet no way to look forward.
Even if it seems like a dream, it's not.
Waking up, the same routine. Do whatever comes to mind.
But still, falling, falling, falling.
Press a button, turn a knob, hold the controller in hand.
Yet falling, falling, falling.
Trying to feel the light, the air, when stranded in an area that has none of that.
Only falling, falling, falling.
But then, a spark, a moment. Soon you and I can see the light we long to see.
Moving out of the world that we stay in.
Now, suddenly, a movement, a run, a swing, a jump, a dream.
Hands rise, eyes close. Suddenly falling is no longer relevant.
Now only rising, rising, rising.
Moving through a field, a desert, a forest, a field, a mountain, even.
There. In the moment. No longer a second behind.
But then, the rising stops.
Rising, rising, rising. Falling, falling, falling.
Waking up. Still here. Still falling.
Still longing to move, to fly, to rise.

George Parckar (12)
Akeley Wood School, Akeley

The Journal

Drip.
Spots of ink dripping slowly onto the blank, white page,
Tainting its purity with sins.
Drip.
I faced him,
The only one who loved us.
Drip.
He turned away from me,
His winged messengers silently following.
Drip.
I was alone.
Cast out and abandoned in this dark cave of my mind.
Mould and dank air suffocating.
Nothing but the deep, empty void and the...
Drip.
Drip.
Drip.
Of my sins.
Crack!
The book slammed shut.
Hope dying with a
Crack.
The bindings snapped.
Footsteps outside my door,
Thundering with my heart as it raced
And the pen hit the desk.

Crack!
Fists on wood,
Crack!
The window wrenched open,
My small, pale hands lying on the sill for a moment,
Before the storm of my soul howled around me.
Books and papers scattered,
Falling like dying stars around me,
Every one marred by the spots of my actions.

Flutter.
A single page leapt past,
Dancing with burning hope as it spun in the turmoil.
My shaking fingers reached out,
Grasping it with a
Rustle.
A chance, a chance the wind screamed,
Writhing as it calmed.
The panic faded while the peace bloomed,
The sunrise after the dreadful night.
Scratch.
The nib danced,
And the footsteps joined,
All while dark ink spilled into words.
The
Scratch.

Like a bird at the window.
The small sound pausing only for a sigh,
As the storm gave way to silence.
Silence.
Save for the...
Scratch
Of my thoughts.
Of pen against paper.
Of the bird finally able to fly.

Madeline White
Akeley Wood School, Akeley

Silverstone In The War

For two years the peaceful village morphed from a slumber,
Silverstone churned out war.
RAF base created,
Bomber command switched on. Fighting hard for our hope!
We will live on!
Turned to an air base the Wellingtons flew.
As the two engines drone out the hardship
We fly and soar to achieve, times are hard.
We will live on!
Many accidents return as many fall.
Pressure is high and bombs descend, descend, descend.
Bomber command is on its way.
We will live on!
As the bombings started, the town's destroyed
What's happening to our country? Life wanted to return.
But at what cost?
Churchill to Chamberlain, we fought hard.
Giving respect to all that departed. 6 years of hard graft.
But all for what?
Lest we forget
The lives we lost.
1939-1945
At what cost?

Kai Purves
Akeley Wood School, Akeley

The Great Escape

I planned each step with careful art,
A daring leap, a quick depart,
From prison walls, I break away,
To taste the dawn of a brand-new day.

The plan is working, I start to run,
I leave the gates, and after a lifetime, I see the sun,
I rush to a halt, gazing at its beauty,
What a sight to see it set, one enormous ball of purity.

I chart my path through stars unseen,
A voyage bold, where none have been,
From shadows deep, I rise anew,
In the vast unknown, I'll find my crew.

I hear somebody call my name,
Fear engulfs but I turn around all the same,
I'm relieved to see my fellow inmate,
I raise my eyebrows; he is quite late.

Smiling we shake hands,
And together we forge our future plans,
We leave the prison, mad memories washed away,
But what has been memorable is this day.

To leave behind the past I know,
And face the future's glowing show,
With courage strong and a heart so free,
I found the path that's meant for me.

Zohan Mohsin
Akeley Wood School, Akeley

Only

There was only ever:
Pink skies, a glittering sun,
An endless sea of lilies,
Dancing with every breeze,
Soft clouds reigning above,
Guarding the gates to eternity.

There was only ever:
That sweet web of white shimmering swirls,
Oh, how lovely it would be to rest,
If only for a moment, an instant,
To close these heavy lids until,
A brush raced across the crisp paper,
As the sharp edge reached out further.

No, there was only ever:
Blue, sparkling butterflies,
Their delicate wings fluttering through,
The sour air, where a metallic tang slowly crept in,
The shard shattered down leaving a crimson stain,
To disfigure the sterile white tiles,
And splatter on the ripped page.

If only there hadn't been,
A soulless grimace in the shadows,
Or hands wiping at a tear-stained face,
Or a pair of dull eyes piercing the wall,
If only they hadn't all been ravaged by their enduring grief.

Ines Gherib
Akeley Wood School, Akeley

Four Days Remain

"We've got less than a week, not two years, Ruth."
Two years feel like two minutes at this point,
No one knows why I love this place so much,
It's more than the fancy clothes and jewellery,
That they bought me, more than nice food,
More than our beautiful rented cottage,
There is no other Ruth in the whole world,
Even if I'm forced to leave them, I'll stay.

They are the ones that shaped my character,
The ones who made all of my dreams come true,
Don't want to end one love for another,
For now, I must choose them or you.

This is where I found love, and now it's almost over,
I can't leave, I mustn't leave, I won't leave.

Joshua MacKinnon
Akeley Wood School, Akeley

Whispers Of Anxiety

In shadows deep, anxiety stands,
A whispering phantom with trembling hands,
It sneaks inside, a fleeting fear,
A silent scream, both far and near.

Heartbeats race like a fleeting gust,
Silent whispers shrouded in dust,
Each breath a struggle, a fight unseen,
Invisible chains, where I have always been.

A weightless burden, it clings so tight,
A sleepless shadow in the quiet night,
With a thousand doubts, and a million 'whys',
Anxiety sings its endless lullabies.

But here we stand, and here we rise,
A flicker of hope in the darkest skies,
With courage, we'll calm the storm within,
And find our peace, where calm begins.

Ollie Chapman
Akeley Wood School, Akeley

Sweet Lily Of The Valley

Sweet lily of the valley,
Surrounded by all that will intimidate.
Your swanned neck, covered by the snake,
As the weeping dew falls in your wake.

Dear lily of the valley,
The walls that surround you are carved out of spite.
Mountains in which surround you with your echo and the call,
Your voice is near cut as they weep and bawl.

Small lily of the valley,
I see your petals have turned and creased.
The wind screeches and shushes you to look away,
So tell me, dear lily, why do you stay?

Sweet lily of the valley,
The walls have plunged straight down.
The shadows once shrieked and wailed,
My dear lily, please leave. For our sake.

Charles Stancliffe-White (16)
Akeley Wood School, Akeley

Take A Chance

Yukimiya sat down on his couch
Crumbs on the floor no doubt
Words flew in his head, what to do tonight?
Sitting down on the couch slumped down, fists thumped, nothing to do with life, why no spirit?
That isn't right
If only he took a chance, destiny could've changed
Pave your own way, don't be afraid
Escape into your mind and you'll be fine
Escape into your positive life and enjoy every little bit.

Jayden Masarira (12)
Akeley Wood School, Akeley

Escape

Sometimes the world feels too loud
Too many voices, too many crowds
So I close my eyes and drift away
To somewhere else, a place that I stay.

It could be a great towering castle or a bottomless pit
Up in the sky above the clouds gazing down
Where my life lies, where I escape, no rules, no work
Just me and my thoughts where no one goes
A hidden place away from the world.

Isaac Kainth
Akeley Wood School, Akeley

Wings Of Valour

In the hush of dawn, engines roar and sigh,
Pilots soar above where eagles fly.
With hearts full of dreams and eyes on the sky,
They chase the horizon where adventures lie.

Clad in uniform, symbol of pride,
Guardians of the skies, with the world as their guide.
Through the storm, through calm, their spirits abide,
With courage unyielding as they take on the tide.

From narrow runways to clouds soft and white,
They navigate realms where earth meets the light.
Each takeoff a promise, each landing a flight,
Defying the limits, embracing height.

With every ascent, they leave fears behind,
In a dance with heaven, they're fiercely enshrined,
The passion ignited, a bond that's defined.

So here's to the pilots, the brave and the true,
With wings of valour, they'll always break through.
In a tapestry woven from skies deep and blue,
They carve out the future with dreams born anew.

Jayden Gomes (15)
Ark Elvin Academy, Wembley

I Have Never Known Peace

Peace is a fantasy,
A dreamland
I can only hope
To visit.

Maybe somewhere,
On the other side of the world,
Children like me,
Take peace for granted.

Maybe somewhere,
On the other side of the world,
Children like me,
Have never slept with missiles as their lullaby.

Never had to walk past
Rock and dust and decay,
Once known as houses,
On their way to school.

That is my reality:
Loss and grief instead of happiness.
Tears and pain instead of laughter.
Darkness and sorrow instead of light.

Where we once played,
Now twisted, sharp memories
Of laughter and innocence,
Of forgotten amusements.

But now, there is nothing but darkness:
All around, the dark of
Crushed walls and spirits encompass
Our very bones.

Threatening
To drown
Our very existence,
A tsunami ravaging our lives.

Funny how
I can say this so... so normally.
We don't even get
Any tourists anymore.

They were driven away
By the prospect of death.
Or maybe it was the fact that
There wasn't anything *left* to tour.

Others would see us and think,
Why didn't they leave when they had the chance?
They wouldn't know the pride
We feel in our home.

They have no right to be here.
This was my father's home, his childhood.
It was my grandfather's home,
And his childhood.

It was my great-grandfather's too.
A land where memories were made and cherished.
Love lost and found,
Where children's laughter echoed off the rafters.

This land is my blood.
So do not be surprised,
Dear invaders,
When we stand our ground.

Do not be surprised when we fight for our land.
Do not be surprised when we fight for our peace.
Do not be surprised when we fight for our people.
Do not be surprised when we fight for our futures.

Do not be surprised when we fight for our freedom.

Rahima Omar
Ark Elvin Academy, Wembley

Imagination Is Important

Imagination is like a key
It can take us places reality can't see
The endless possibilities set us free
In a world that's ours to simply be
So why not explore this concept with me?

Together we can create a dreamland
Where skies are yellow, and the plants
Where the beaches are funky, with pink sand
It's silly, I know! But that's what it's for
It's like opening distant, new doors!

The skies stretch out far and wide
That's where the magic hides!
Within the cotton clouds
As it dances to the rhythm of the wind
Now, as I bring this poem to a close
I hope you realise that those
Who can spark creativity
Twinkle like stars in the night
Oh, how they glow so bright
Good day to you all and goodnight.

Shinaya Robinson
Ark Elvin Academy, Wembley

The Mirage

In a place we all once visited,
Where good memories proceed astray,
Where summer feels like winter,
Like sometimes how joy goes away

In an abandoned desert,
Where no trees grow,
And the rays of sunlight,
Make it the only light that glows

The evening slices the sun in half,
As the sky turns amethyst,
As you mitigate your disturbing mind,
You check the time on your wrist

As the majestic night falls,
The pale moon lights the eventide,
As nature's lullaby lulls you to sleep,
You feel mistaken inside

As your eyes drift open,
You see light in the dark,
Something burns inside you,
Like a thousand fires lit by one spark

Your mind goes through nostalgia,
You descend through the abyss,
As you break your fall,
You feel a peaceful bliss

As you wake up, panting,
You realise it was a trance,
As you begin to breathe,
Your realisation begins to enhance

Eyes full of tears,
Beautiful when it gleams,
Venture out in the world,
Opportunities it teems

Remember building forts,
And playing outside,
And doodling masterpieces
Or stabbing a rubber alongside

Remember when we ate the cookies,
And then we would have lied,
Or take naps for hours,
Guess our inner child just died

In a place we all once visited,
Where memories never camouflage,
Where winter feels like summer,
Where life feels like a mirage

-Mirage

Aleeza Chaudhery (12)
Ark Elvin Academy, Wembley

The Shadow We Share

Racism, a shadow cast deep and wide,
A wound in the heart that no love can hide.
It rises in silence; it speaks in the air,
A poison that lingers, that festers, that tears.

It builds walls between, it silences truth,
It robs us of kindness, of innocence, of youth.
It feeds on division, on what we perceive,
On colour and culture, on what we believe.

But we are all threads in a vast woven quilt,
Each pattern and shade, each hand that was built.
Our strength lies in difference, in stories untold,
In hearts that untie, in hands that unfold.

So let us break chains, let our voices be clear,
No more will we whisper, no more will we fear.
For love knows no borders, no colour, no race,
It thrives in the warmth of the human embrace.

Sarah-Alexandra Dulgheriu (12)
Ark Elvin Academy, Wembley

Echoes Of Resilience

In Gaza's ground, where shadows sigh
Beneath a blood-red bitter sky
The winds like wailing spirits weep
And in their cry the promises sleep

Through endless wars and wounding plight,
The people stand, though bruised by night
Their courage carved in every stone,
Their spirits whisper, fiercely grown,

The bombs like beasts with thunder tear
The walls once proud, now gasping air
Yet through the chaos, through the flame
Palestine remains, unbowed, its name.

In olive groves the past persists
Where ancient hands still grasp and twist
The roots like fingers, grasp the ground
Defiant, though the world resounds

For in their veins, the rivers flow
Of battles fought, of endless woe,
Yet brighter still their hearts ignite,
For justice, truth, they claim their right

The world may turn, may close its eyes,
To silent screams beneath the skies.
But Gaza's heart, with beating bold,
Will rise and fight, and break the cold,

Let cannons roar, let smoke arise,
The ash like ghosts will fill the skies,
Yet Palestine with fires alight,
Will rise again and claim its right.

For not in steel, nor swords' sharp grin,
But in the will that burns within –
The soul of Palestine, unbound,
A land that rises from the ground.

In every breath, in every tear,
They chase away their darkest fear,
A nation born of flame and stone,
Palestine, forever known...

Waleed Ibrahemi
Ark Elvin Academy, Wembley

Life's Story

Stories behold; stories be told,
Myths and legends, yet none could compare to the story we bear,
Each unique, with a tale to tell,
With war and gore,
Nonetheless, we try our best,
Racism, bullying, ignorance and neglect,
All this disrespect,
Liberate this world from pure injustice,
And bring to all the world,
We require a utopia amidst chaos – these unending flaws,
Escape the chains of anxiety and expectations,
And come to terms with your reality,
Perfection is impossible,
But we strive for the best,
We are our dreams to become the best,
Doubting and stupidity hold us back but like a slingshot,
We must shoot back to the cosmos high and the sun, the sky,
Beyond our 'limits', beyond what everyone thought was impossible,
We prove time and time again that when we are united,
We are a force of nature,
In history, we prevailed, so can we not again end this world's problems,
And unite as one force and never be separated again into war and conflict?

Can one die in such a miserable state?
No. One, one thing must be great,
So, should we strive to the skies and answer the question that has existed since the beginning of time:
As humans, can we really be one?
With no war and fight, no gore and night?
Let us answer this question by giving each one of our stories,
Even if you believe that you did something horrid,
Your life is still worth it, no matter the story.

Rovito Da Costa (11)
Ark Elvin Academy, Wembley

Wabi-Sabi

Wabi-sabi – that's the word,
They aren't imperfections – that word's just absurd,
So read this now and when you look in the mirror and see you,
You won't go "Ew" – because you were never ugly – who lied to you?

Scars – "You look crazy! How do you survive with scars?"
False! Each one is a beautiful, shining star!
Moles and beauty spots! "Are you mutated?"
I have plenty too! Rated them ten out of ten for me and you!

Too skinny? "Ew, ew, ew!"
It's beautiful and you know it too!
Too chubby? "Really?" you say,
You are amazing! They can't ruin your day!

Wait a minute! There is another wabi-sabi too!
Not just beauty in people but also in things,
Anything! From a rusty ring to a crack on the wall or a dirty shoe!

We must accept the transience,
And create a positive ambience!
The gorgeous, unique, incomplete nature,
Put that in a highlighted box – it's major!

So next time you see anything –
Object or person,
It has imperfections that make,
It as stunning as a ruby – if not more!
Now you know what wabi-sabi is,
And add some to your life and see!

Mila Johnson (12)
Ark Elvin Academy, Wembley

Racism Poem

In a world of hues a vibrant array,
Where colours dance and spirits sway,
A shadow falls, a chilling blight,
Racism's sting, a cruel dark night.
It whispers lies, divides and tears,
Planting seeds of doubt and fears,
Judging souls by shades of skins,
Where hatred's grip begins to win.
It paints a world in black and white,
Robbing heart of joy and light.
Blind to beauty, deaf to grace,
Leaving scars upon our face.
But let us rise with voices strong,
Singing songs right from wrong,
Rejecting hate's insidious call,
Building bridges, standing tall,
But in our hearts, the fire burns,
A yearning for a world that learns.
That's love's embrace, a boundless sea,
Transcends all shades, wild and free.

Zoha Nouman-Chohan (11)
Ark Elvin Academy, Wembley

Why Me?

My father lies in a pool of blood
In front of me.

I never knew that I would see him like this.
I never knew I would find myself like this.
I never knew that it could come to this.
I never knew anything, really.

So why is it my soul that's being torn apart?
Why is it me amongst many children on this battlefield?
Why is it me amidst the grenades, rifles and ammunition?
And why not you?

Why is it me in my third-world country
And you in your first?
Why has my throat been wrung dry
Whilst yours has experienced a sip of some herbal tea?
Why am I crying out for God
While you're questioning Him?

Why is this my reality
And that
Yours?

Angel Gracias (16)
Ark Elvin Academy, Wembley

Dust Of Stars, Ash Of Men

Society, the art of law
Prevents a tragic flaw
Avoids the abuse of power
The crucial safety of our

Society, the home of learning
In future we hope for great earning
Halls filled with knowledge
Let our success be acknowledged

Peace isn't sustained
Battles and swords bloodstained
Wounds and scars
People left behind bars

Kids abandoned
Lives destroyed
Homes untouched
Hearts crushed

The sun, a fiery flame
The moon, lots of fame
The Milky Way, full of light
Space! Oh, so bright

Saturn with the ring of honour
Space, there's nothing ever so calmer
Moons orbiting
Stars sparkling.

Samaira Manha
Ark Elvin Academy, Wembley

A Fate Undeserved

I hold a still corpse of one so young,
Once filled with a passionate fire,
But now snuffed out,
Lies just a pile of bones and dust,
That makes my eyes sting,
As debris rests on my lashes

Debris that used to be part of a home,
But now a house,
A body that deserved a chance at life,
But was subjected to human nature,
They said they would save us from our religion,
But is safety the smell of smoke and flesh?
Cries and shrieks that echo in one's ears?
Wounds that only ever seem to partially heal,
Words that never seem to disappear after leaving the mouth,
Eyes that have seen everything but yet know nothing.
Is our only way to safety, death?

Maryam Hussain (12)
Ark Elvin Academy, Wembley

Dementia Alzheimer's Society

My truth is an illness
That affects the brain
Forgets people's names
Forgets the train
Or thoughts that came
Dementia is not a game
UK's number one killer
It's all pain
People complain
And suffer as it began
Like a book shell
Everything falls apart
Especially the family's heart
Hearing uncured illness
That tears me apart
Spreading awareness
But are you aware?
Deaths are coming anyway,
Old or young,
Is nothing to play
But don't worry with £1,000
We will show love and support
Win or not
Nothing to worry about, spread awareness before it touches your heart.

Fatma Al Enazy
Ark Elvin Academy, Wembley

Untitled

Restless clouds in my mind
Thundering and raining
Yet streets are dried
And people are still weeping.

Despite the drought
The people get by
Swept the brush
Some are harsher than others
But yet we've wept
Only to have no reaction.

Days where I sleep
Or I can see the blue sky
I imagine a glass city
A mist to a violent sand
Or desolate lakes
However, if it had existed
Thou wilt not know
Shrouded by fumes
Thou art breathed unto life.

Prince Golgis Musemina (15)
Ark Elvin Academy, Wembley

Palestine

From the river to the sea,
Palestine should be free,
From our hearts and above,
Palestine should be loved,
From the sky to space,
There should be no struggles
Palestinians should face,
From the ocean to below,
Palestine should be known,
From the soil to the sand,
Palestine wants their land,
From the grass to the trees,
Palestine should be seen.

Aicha El Gallaf-Ajiyel
Ark Elvin Academy, Wembley

Untitled

The sun is a star,
So beautiful yet so far,
It gives us light,
And it is one of my favourite stars that I really like,
The moon is a ray,
That we see at the end of the day,
When the shadows lengthen and come out to play,
The stars are like diamonds,
Twinkling so bright,
They fill us with wonder,
In the darkness of the night.

Selven D'Silva
Ark Elvin Academy, Wembley

Where The Rain Lives

I find myself where the rain lives,
In all it takes and all it gives,
Washing away the fears unseen
Blurring reality and my dreams.

Each droplet calls out loudly to me,
"Go, be free of this misery,"
But the desperate cries cannot be heard
Over the wings of the messenger bird.

The rain muffles the drumming pace,
Of the boy who's got to face
The sad truth of the world today,
But through the pain he's got to play.

My eyes tear up with every drop,
Every heart that comes to a stop,
Though I dream of a better home,
Bullets fly through the skies unknown.

So if you hear the drone of rain,
Think about our collective pain,
For in every drop, every beat,
They send out another fleet.

Faiza Safi (15)
Bentley Wood High School, Stanmore

Unseen

The scroll's endless parade of faces blurred and bright,
Perfect smiles, a hollow ache in the chest,
Pounding head, the whisper, *not enough*, a constant fight,
Against the pressure, a crushing, unseen test.

Breath catches, a ragged gasp in the dark,
Insomnia's cruel lies, a seed of doubt has grown,
The mirror shows a stranger, a broken, fractured mark,
Who am I supposed to be, lost and unknown?

I close my eyes and dream of open skies,
A field of wildflowers, swaying in the breeze,
No filters, no judgments, just the sun that lies,
Warm on my skin, a moment of sweet ease.

Freedom is a word that tastes like air so clean,
And smells like a possibility, a world untold,
I want to run, beyond the screen,
And breathe, and be, a story to unfold.

The worn pages of a book, a world to find,
Music that vibrates, a symphony of the soul,
Solitude's quiet comfort, my own peace of mind,
The woods stand tall, and strong, making me whole.

Treasures unseen, they cannot touch or claim,
A small rebellion, deleting the endless feed,
My eyes in the mirror, I whisper my own name,
My beauty, my success, my story, my own creed.

Not perfect, but real, and finally, truly mine,
I breathe, and I begin, a future I define.

Sara Shahood (13)
Bentley Wood High School, Stanmore

To You, The Sun

You are the lantern in my unlit corridors,
A friend that lifts the dusk from my skies.
I am a silhouette, fractured and fading,
But your light etches wholeness where shadow lies.

Your words are rivers carving stone,
A quiet power eroding despair.
Each glance you offer is an untouched dawn,
A reminder that brokenness still breathes air.

While I, the unsteady earth, collapse beneath storms –
You are constellations, constant and sure.
Even in the hollow, I name my heart,
Your presence plants what may one day endure.

I love you as the moon loves the sea:
From a distance, in tides I cannot embrace –
Your friendship hangs stars in my darkest void,
An eternal horizon in an unwelcome place.

Mya Ali (15)
Bentley Wood High School, Stanmore

Keep Moving

The moment arrives - you sit, you stare,
You gasp for breath, yet none is there,
The ticking clock pounds on you without care,
A test begins - you're unprepared!

Your mind is blank, your hands feel tight,
Your heartbeat drums despite your might,
A hundred eyes are in the room,
Whilst a silent storm builds up inside of you.

You grip your pen and take your aim,
You fight to focus, but in pain,
The numbers twist, they leap, they fade,
Like echoes lost in hollow shade.

The clock moves on, it never waits,
You're bound within this tangled fate,
You're trapped within this never-ending maze,
Though strength is forged on days like these.

Jasmine Gioiosa (13)
Bentley Wood High School, Stanmore

Escape

I'm afraid
It's hard to escape
I was tip-top, now I'm out of shape
You're not here anymore and I need your aid.

It's unfair
Chances of escaping are lean
My best memory of you plays like a movie scene
And it gets hard to breathe in the air.

It's improving
I can escape for longer
I've gotten stronger
But you're still there and you're not leaving.

I'm progressing
I'm able to escape almost eternally
However, you're a memory locked away internally
But you still claw your way into my thoughts and it has me stressing.

I know you're with me
Even if you're not in front of me.

Ruqaiya Mohamed Jinnah (13)
Bentley Wood High School, Stanmore

Roots Beneath The Ruin

In the iron jaws where silence breaks,
The earth drinks the blood it takes.
Shattered voices, a distant hum,
Dreams undone by the beating drum.
Fields once golden turned to ash,
Lives are spent in power's clash.
The vultures wait, the shadows spread,
As sorrow blooms where greed is fed.
A hollow crown, a poisoned feast,
Men are pawns and war's the beast.
But beneath the rubble, roots will rise,
Hope still burns beneath the lies.
Let the sun unmask the lie
That glory lives where children die.
A world rebuilt where scars can heal,
And peace becomes the truest steel.

Alyah Ibrahim Mohamed (16)
Bentley Wood High School, Stanmore

My Secret Garden Of Joy

In my secret garden,
There are many sights to behold
From the busy buzzing bees
To the happily swaying trees

My secret garden can be anything I imagine
It can have monkeys
It can have clunky shoes
Walking around as they please
There can be bright yellow blocks of cheese!

Just to be clear,
This is not what it's like
But rather calm and peaceful

I can grow things
Anything you can think of!

It is my place, only for me
To relax in my mind
And rest and rest!

Mia Pindoria (12)
Bentley Wood High School, Stanmore

Untitled

This time we fell
Through storm, fire, and rain
We held and remained
Through eruptions and tremblers
We held, we stayed strong
Through shockers and rumblers
We held on

But this time we fell
Through the angelic arms of death
We fell, let go
Encased in a beautiful disaster.

Anniyah Sethi (14)
Bentley Wood High School, Stanmore

Death

Death is always hunting you
Haunting you
Always there
Death

It's the man in the black cloak
The Grim Reaper
The Devil
Death
Hunting you
Haunting you
Death is around the corner
It is coming for you
Seizing every chance to kill you

It's the smog in the air
It's the black cloud billowing from a factory
Death
Is coming for you
Always out to get you
Catch you off guard

Hunting you
Haunting you
Death is around the corner
Seizing every chance to grab you and murder you
Prepare to die

Death
Death is there for you
Getting ready to destroy you off the face of this Earth

Whether at sea or on land
It will find a way to send you to Davy Jones' locker
On land it will pull you to the centre of the Earth
Die, die
Die, die
Death is yours
Oh Death

Death is hunting you
Haunting you
Death is around the corner
Death is prominent
It is waiting patiently for you to kick the bucket and die
Death wants to destroy you

Death, death
Waiting to eliminate you
Waiting for you to pop your clogs
It is so strong when you're weak
Death
Death
Die die dieeeeee!

Theo Heritage (11)
Bexhill Academy, Bexhill-On-Sea

Just A Kid

I'm trapped under a boulder,
And I want to get out,
But they won't let me,
At least, not until I'm older.

Who's 'they', you might be wondering,
Well I'll tell you right now.
It's just adults in general.
I'm stuck in their cage,
And I want to get out.

I'm going to let you in on a secret,
Promise you won't tell?
Us kids are sick and tired,
Of being locked in your cell.

No, we don't want your assistance,
We can do it on our own,
And can you please just stop,
Belittling our existence.

Because I do know stuff,
And I can do quite a lot.
I'm not 'just a kid',
I'm loads more than that.

I'm a human being,
With my own opinions.
I have a voice,
And yes, I can make my own decisions.

So this is a message,
To all the adults out there,
We should be valued,
And our thoughts should be shared.

Jessica Wilson (12)
Bexhill Academy, Bexhill-On-Sea

An Escape Route

I'm a robot
Waiting to be controlled
Easy to shut down
Except with one wrong move
I could be gone forever

My mind acts like a volcano
Ready to erupt at any second
As if I'm a single flame
That will eventually dry out

I feel confined
Though I'm surrounded by people
I lose myself so easily
Drowning in thoughts
I'm in the winter too deep to come back now

Maybe I'm fighting my own war
If it ends another will begin
I envy those at peace

I wonder if some days will be different
Where I'm not recorded by cameras
Where I can escape my shadow
Then I wake up from the dream

Anxiety permanently lingers over my back
I can feel it whispering
I can hear it breathing
Telling me that I'm the key
But not which way to turn.

Lucia McDermott (12)
Bexhill Academy, Bexhill-On-Sea

Ignorance Is Bliss

In this world where ignorance is bliss
You'll never truly realise all the nasty comments you've missed.
When given a gift to see through one's eyes
It'll be lies which would eventually lead to your demise.
I walk through this life and look around,
There's nothing precious,
Nothing to be found.
When you can see through one's true nature,
Nothing feels real,
Maybe it's me who I want to kid,
But if I die I'll never be able to smile,
Never be able to cry
And never be able to soar through the never-ending sky.
I'm trapped, no I'm running,
Running from this curse,
I won't just stand there and let it get worse.
I, Enola, have always been alone but not today,
I'll pick up the phone, dial a number
And awake from this eternal slumber
And be free, be truly me.

Zoe Ogechi Nwuju (12)
Bexhill Academy, Bexhill-On-Sea

The Place Where I Want To Be

I stood on the edge of it all,
The city behind me, big and small.
I left the streets for open skies,
Where dreams feel real and hopes can rise.

The roads grew quiet, the noise grew thin,
I stepped outside and looked within.
I followed the path where the pavement ends,
To open fields and forest bends.

The rivers danced as they ran so free,
The wind sang softly, just for me.
The trees stood tall, the hills so still,
A place of calm, a place of will.

No walls, no rush, no heavy plans,
Just open skies and open lands.
I found a space to breathe, to grow,
A place where joy begins to show.

The stars at night fell bright and near,
A quiet sky without a fear.
This is my home, my soul, my way,
Where every moment shapes my day.

Ben Ashby (12)
Bexhill Academy, Bexhill-On-Sea

It's Okay To Not Be Okay

I remind myself,
It's okay to not be okay,
I try to escape,
And allow myself time,
I need to escape it one day.

I remind myself,
To be kind to myself,
It's okay to have anxiety,
It's okay to be scared,
It's okay to worry,
Don't think negatively,
Because you are not a failure,
Until you try...
I need to escape it one day.

I remind myself,
To take a deep breath,
And remember,
It's okay to not be okay,
There is no shame,
I need to escape it one day,
That day is today.

Myah Wapples (11)
Bexhill Academy, Bexhill-On-Sea

Escape The Mind

School.
It hurt for many of us.
Including me.
The negativity just flows to me.
Like a waterfall.
It hurts.

They laugh all day.
The laughter burns.
They reach my phone while I'm at home.
I want to escape.
But there is no escape.

Every day gets worse.
More hurting.
More burns.
Until I crack.

I reach out.
They help.
Days get better.
I have escaped...

Fraya Vaillant (12)
Bexhill Academy, Bexhill-On-Sea

Maze Of The Heart

If I could escape,
I would go to my safe space.
In a future utopia,
Where I was home.

Away from my family,
And school expectations.
Chained and alone,
Like a prisoner in a dungeon.

But if there was freedom,
My anxiety would go.
Open and no stress,
Escaped and no problems.

If I could only escape,
My life would be changed.
But that takes a miracle,
And I am no God…

Natalia Nowicka (12)
Bexhill Academy, Bexhill-On-Sea

Welcome To My World

Welcome to my world,
A world you can't escape,
A world full of bad thoughts,
Sadness, anxiety, stress.

Welcome to my world,
No one to help,
No safe place,
Darkness, fear, alone.

Welcome to my world,
Freedom has vanished,
Freedom has run away,
Empty grave, so much hate.

Welcome to my world,
You're stuck in one place,
You're stuck forever,
Trapped, stuck, can't escape.

Chloe Lazenby (12)
Bexhill Academy, Bexhill-On-Sea

Summer

One day, when the flowers bloom,
And the sun brightens,
Then the wind gets less annoying
But then you realise...
It's summer.

The pool comes out,
Splashing about,
In summer,
In summer.

Mums and dads get drenched in the pool,
Because children mess about.

Time goes by, it's getting dark,
"Out of the pool!" Mum says.

Daisy Wright (11)
Bexhill Academy, Bexhill-On-Sea

Thoughts, Our Sole Power

When you want to say something,
Think, what you say could inspire them
Or hurt them for the rest of their lives.

Before putting an empty bag in the trash
Check first what's in the bag.

As Emily Dickinson once said:
"The brain is wider than the sky
Will there be room to think about your words?"

Antonio Peteoaca (12)
Bexhill Academy, Bexhill-On-Sea

The Mask We Wear

We smile in crowds, with eyes closed tight,
A fragile facade to hide the fight.
Behind the curve of lips we press,
Lies a heart burdened with distress.

The world sees joy, a gleam, a spark,
But inside, we're trembling in the dark.
The mask is perfect, flawless, bright,
Hiding the scars we dare not cite.

We laugh, we joke, we carry on,
Pretending life's a game we've won.
Yet under layers, deep within,
A storm is brewing, soaked in sin.

The cracks begin to show, so faint,
A twitch, a flinch, a trace of restraint.
But still, we stand, we never fall,
The mask intact, despite it all.

For fear of what they'll think or say,
We choose to wear the lie each day.
Hiding the tears that streak our face,
Concealing grief with fleeting grace.

But in the quiet, when alone,
The mask slips off, the truth is known.
We are not strong, we are not whole,
Just lost and wandering, aching souls.

Yet still we wear the mask with pride,
To fool the world, and to collide
With every lie, every disguise,
Hoping one day we'll realise,

That we are more than what we show,
That in our hearts, we also grow –
Not just the pain, but strength as well,
For even masks, one day fell.

Charlie Meredith (14)
Birchgrove Comprehensive School, Birchgrove

Jenga

Life is like a tower of Jenga
Each block holds another.
Relying on one another
To create a platform.
Reliable for balance and
Stable for life to thrive.

But, like a Jenga tower
Our lives are pulled down by society.
Pulling out our blocks until
We can no longer
Hold ourselves up.

One by one our towers
Are pulled down as the game is played.
Block by block, we lose ourselves.

Don't lose your blocks
Hold them as they hold you
Don't lose the game.

Jasper Higgitt (13)
Birchgrove Comprehensive School, Birchgrove

Forget About The Past

In the forest deep, where shadows rest,
A campfire flickers, a traveller's test,
The wind hums low, a whispered plea,
Calling the lost to the arms of the trees.

The pines stand silent, strong and wise,
Their branches tracing forgotten skies,
Each leaf a whisper, each breeze a guide,
Urging the restless to leave pain behind.

Once, there were voices, bright as the day,
Laughter like rivers, then fading away,
Time pulled the threads, unravelling fast,
Leaving ghosts in the echoes of the past.

But the forest does not clutch or grieve,
It sheds its burdens like autumn leaves,
The fire may burn with memories old,
Yet its warmth spins stories still untold.

So follow the trails where the wild winds call,
Let the trees rise high and the past grow small,
For nature knows what the lost hearts do,
Escape is not leaving, but starting anew.

Dur Zanib (15)
Bolton Muslim Girls' School, Bolton

Shackled

Cold like day. Warm like night.
Bright like shadows. Dim like light.
It hurts, this darkness that blankets all –

Swallowing
Soothing.

It muffles my agonised sobs that break the tranquil quiet.
But I've finally learnt to control the riot.
It hurts, these Songs of Silence that are so loud –

Powerful
Melancholy.

It masks the cheer and bustle outside the cage,
I've tried to reach out to it, but it's been an age.
It hurts, being so close yet so far –

Taunting
Reassuring.

It engulfs the brightness that interrupts this stygian constraint,
I tried to erase it, but in vain.
It hurts, this light that refuses to reach the corners of my mind –

Luminous
Dim.

It does not break even when I struggle,
This chain.
Sharp sonorous sound,
Cascades and rings and echoes and screams
Bounce off walls.
A rising crescendo
A falling orchestra.

It hurts, that laughter that only reverberates and
resonates in the back of my cell,
A faint, fading memory
Of sunny smiles and sunny days
That I once relished
But are left as only that –
Memories.

I yearn to feel it once again,
That thrumming life that has died,
Buried
Coffined.
Restless sleep. Concealed in my
Empty heart.

I pray, I wish, I long, I dream,
I hope to break the shackles of the cage that is my
Mind.

Arfa Imran (15)
Bolton Muslim Girls' School, Bolton

Whispers Of A Silent Storm

I stand where shadows meet the ground,
A shudder in the air, without a sound.
Fear, like a chain, wraps tight around my chest,
A constant ache, a heart never at rest.

Neglect isn't loud, it's the silence that stings,
A child's cry drowned by the sound of broken wings.
Where hope is stolen, and love is betrayed,
The warmth of a mother no longer stays.

Ignorance blinds us with its veil,
We walk through life, so numb, so frail.
We see the tears, but choose to look away,
Comforted in the lies we choose to say.

War is not a battle fought by hand,
It's the destruction of dreams, the blood on the lands,
Children cry where hope no longer grows,
As the world turns a blind eye to all it owes.

Inequality lies beneath the skin,
A gaping wound we cannot begin,
To heal with words, or mend with time,
For we built the world with bitter crime.

Trust is lost, like a broken thread,
Words are empty, hearts are dead,
No one believes, no one will stand,
As we watch the world falls out of our hands.

This world is broken, fractured deep,
We live in pain and misery, while the powerful and rich sleep,
And though we cry, they turn away,
As if our lives don't matter anyway.

I will not be silenced, nor forget,
The pain we live in, the debt we've met,
So hear me out, as I scream the names,
Of every soul that suffers in pain.

Haram Arfan (12)
Bolton Muslim Girls' School, Bolton

Retreat Into Dreamland

When the world feels hard, I close my eyes
And fly to a place where happiness lies.
The sky is bright, the air is clear,
Everything I love is waiting here.

No clocks, no worries, no race to win,
Just quiet moments, peace within.
The rivers shine, the trees all sway,
In Dreamland, it's always a perfect day.

The stars come out to light my way,
They tell me stories, they laugh, they play.
The moon smiles down and hums a tune,
A song of hope beneath its glow so soon.

In Dreamland, the world feels kind and free,
A place that's made for you and me.
I build my home with love and care,
In Dreamland, I can go anywhere.

So when the world feels dark and grey,
I close my eyes and drift away
To Dreamland, where the colours gleam,
A perfect world inside my dream.

Tehreem Zia (11)
Bolton Muslim Girls' School, Bolton

The Night Sky

Stars appeared in the night sky,
As twinkling diamonds shone.
The thought made me want to fall into slumber.
It was luminous in the night sky,
Glistening in sparkling fireworks,
And of course, more stunning than ever.
Clouds drifted past as if in a spectacular dream world.
What are the secrets you hold?
Tell me all that remains untold.
Moonlight's embrace, so gentle and warm,
Guides you to rest away from the storm.
No matter how far away from a loved one,
You will always see the same moon.
I love the fact that the moon is imperfect, but still shines.
Not every moon belongs to our sky.
When the season of shooting stars begins,
It is like a miracle that has been placed upon us.
The first star is always the brightest.
How I love the night sky.

Ayesha Faisal (11)
Bolton Muslim Girls' School, Bolton

Under The Veil Of Occupation

The sky once was blue, now contaminated with smoke.
As the world turned its back, the spirit of the people broke.
For lives have been lost, and hearts have been shattered.
The streets, once filled with children's laughter.
Now it echoes with grief, what a haunting after.
Through jagged rubble and bloodied debris.
Anticipating that people would finally see.
Where dates grew, where life once grew.
Concealed now by a bloodstained hue.
Their eyes filled with misery and fear.
Praying to god, for it all to disappear.
Hoping for light the depths below.
Every breath is laced with woe.

Through the darkness, their path is clear.
Filled with hope, the end is near.
Voices muted, longing to be free.
A land denied its right to be.

Aisha Ahmed (13)
Bolton Muslim Girls' School, Bolton

All In One

She is the strength that holds me steady
She is the sweetness that softens every sorrow
She is the best, my heart's true compass
The one who makes my life worth.

My mum is the best teacher
She taught me how to speak
She taught me how to walk
She taught me how to write.

My mum is my best friend
She supports me in my good decisions
She corrects me if I am wrong
She stays beside me in my tough times.

My mum is the best part of my world
The soul of my every joy, who supports me
Loves me, and guides me to the right path.
She is the first one to wake and the
Last one to rest.

Anika Mehjaben (14)
Bolton Muslim Girls' School, Bolton

World War II

Terrifying tanks, struggling soldiers,
Battling bullets – all this fills soldiers with sadness.
They were ready but scared,
Yet brothers in arms were prepared.

As all the noises of bombs echoed in their ears loudly,
The fearless hearts of stone stood proudly.
They stood there, watching the end coming,
As every tear from them meant something.

Rain of booming bombs,
The fearless fighters are fighting for us.
Bullets are flying high in the skies,
Lighting up like fireflies.

Did they kill the enemies,
Or did they kill men with families?
Family members had thoughts and fears,
As the bombs cascaded down like their tears.

Afiyah Pathan (11)
Bolton Muslim Girls' School, Bolton

A Heart Left Behind

In a world where smiles often lie,
I've learned to watch the fleeting sky,
False faces flicker, friendships fade,
Empty words in shadows laid.

Family's warmth, a distant glow,
Familiar hands that let me go,
Unspoken words hang in the air,
Echoes of love that isn't there.

I wear a mask cold and strong,
A silence where my heart belongs,
Feelings buried, locked away,
Afraid of what might slip and stray.

A heart that knows the weight of night,
Of being alone, yet out of sight,
I stand apart, yet long to be,
A stranger still, even to me.

Damil Arfan (14)
Bolton Muslim Girls' School, Bolton

The Voices In My Head...

The voices keep talking,
Their words swirl around in my head,
They tell me I'm weak,
They tell me I'm scared,
Their words come out like giant grizzly bears,
Their words attack my mind
With their sharp claws and teeth,
I want to scream,
I want to shout, "Help!"
I want to escape,
Escape from this world full of doubt.

Here in my mind,
There is no warmth of the sun,
There are no puppies,
Or cute teddy bears,
I have nothing,
Nothing to hug,
Nothing to squeeze,
Nothing to comfort me while I sleep.

People say I'm strong,
People say I'm brave,
They think my life is perfect,
But they don't hear the voices,
They don't see the tears in my eyes,

They just don't see how they affect me,
Their minds don't feel the sharp claws and teeth.

I want to scream,
I want to shout, "Help!"
But I realise there's no escaping,
There's no escaping the sharp claws and teeth,
There's no escaping or relief from the voices,
The voices that swirl around in my head,
They tell me I'm weak,
They tell me I'm scared,
But maybe they're right,
Because my mind isn't prepared,
It isn't prepared for the path laid ahead,
It isn't prepared to deal with the voices...

They cave in,
And in,
Until my mind collapses,
Until I scream,
I can't do it anymore,
I can't take the growing pressure,
I can't live with the voices!

But I can only shout it in my head,
Where no one can hear me,
Where no one can tell me I'm wrong,
That my feelings are wrong,

That it's all in my head,
I'm weak and I'm scared,
The voices were right...
I'm not prepared.

Reese Lane-Mudie (13)
Caldicot School, Caldicot

Expectations

Every day feels like a fight,
A battle between what's wrong and what's right
Society has standards, it has higher expectations
But no one will ever reach the top, the light.
The world feels like a messed-up creation,
No one ever takes responsibility for their actions.

They *expect* the 'less superior' ones to deal with it all,
They *expect* us all to get on with our daily lives,
They *expect* us to pretend that nothing bad is happening in the world when it is.

It makes us feel disheartened,
It makes us feel like we are not heard,
It makes us feel like no one cares about what we think or want to say,
It makes us feel stupid for feeling worried about what might come next.
What if we helped each other?
What if we put in the effort to understand everyone's struggles?
What if we addressed and sorted out all the problems and issues that we are facing in the world today?
It may take a while, but it will be worth it,
We can't stay silent anymore.
We need to work to get to be able to make a better tomorrow.

Jessica Hobbs (8)
Caldicot School, Caldicot

Untitled

I am not a word
I am loud and expressive and not made to be understood
I will not be clay
I will not grow smaller to fit your mould
Just because I have an identity does not mean it is all I am
Just because I am not understood does not mean I am not understandable

I am merely trying to live
But, it is hard to live happily when all you are known by is what you are not
To be treated normally when you yourself are obviously not feels impossible
Belonging turns into a dream when you are so different to those you see, hear, look up to
As if you are the only one in the world who is broken in this way
The minutes feel like hours trying to figure out why you don't fit in the box you were put in
Until you see yourself as more whole for it
Until you find those few,
The ones who feel the same way
The ones who know you as you are, not who you were or how you are seen, who you are
When you find them the world seems more on your side
The ones who stood against you don't stand as tall

When you know you are right by your own knowing or
intervention it is easier to stand against what is wrong
It is easier to be yourself when you are not constantly being
told you are wrong for it
So stop telling people they are wrong for who they are, if
there is no harm in it let them be
What is so hard about letting people be?

Eli Bruce (13)
Caldicot School, Caldicot

The Weight Of Silence

I feel this weight, it's deep inside,
A storm of thoughts I cannot hide.
I hate myself; I can't explain,
But telling someone feels like pain.

What if they see me as weak or wrong?
What if they don't hear or think I don't belong?
I keep it hidden, locked away,
Afraid of the judgment they might say.

I want to break free, but the chains won't snap,
I don't know where to go. Should I turn back?
The silence grows louder; it's all I've ever known,
I hate that I continue to feel so alone.

Forever on and on, I continue circling,
A hollow path, the void is beckoning.
No voice, no light, just endless falling,
The quiet consumes, an eternal stalling.

I wish to be normal, to blend, to belong,
But the weight of this fight feels endlessly wrong.
The silence screams louder than I can cope,
Longing for a way to just feel hope.

I bury my thoughts, too dark to say,
A heart full of sorrow led astray.
The silence inside is all I hear,
A never-ending battle with my fear.

In shadows deep, I watch myself fall,
A prisoner to my self-made wall.
A mirror cracked, reflecting pain,
Where once was hope, now only rain.

Why can't it stop? Why can't I break free?
If I tell someone, they won't believe me.

Lexi Connolly (12)
Caldicot School, Caldicot

Inside Is Perfect

Inside is perfect, but outside is not
The world is burning, the air feels hot.
Wars rage on and oceans rise
The future fades before my eyes.

Outside they argue, they fight, they destroy.
My dreams unravel and there is no more joy.
People in power set the world ablaze,
Leaving me to deal with the smoke and the haze.

Inside my mind, there's a world I have made,
Where the scars of the earth have begun to fade.
In my imagination, there is no war, no fear,
Just harmony and peace, but I don't think it's near.

Everyone's equal, there's food for all.
No borders, no hate, no need for any war.
The forests are green, the skies are blue,
Inside my dreams, the world is renewed.

Outside is quickly falling apart,
A world so broken, it's tearing my heart.
I want to shout, to make them see
But all I have left is this dream inside of me.

Inside is perfect, though outside is not,
Maybe someday I will fix what they forgot.
Until then, I will keep dreaming of the world we could be,
Where love conquers hate and everyone's free.

Ffion Davies
Caldicot School, Caldicot

Ode To The Rueful

Elastic around my lungs is arresting again,
Heads hung down, full of remorse.
You're just a kid, you know,
Negatives attach to you like you're a strong force,
Neglected, unusual souls.

Detach your head when you feel forsaken,
Fathom the truth that their point of view is mistaken.
Your mind is hollow, and your bed is numb,
No more nothingness, what's done is done.

You see that glimpse in the corner of the room,
Stare in the face of danger and impending doom.
Please understand that it's only a spark,
But only a spark is how the fireworks start.

Run from the hills to the fields with your friends,
Engulfing a book that never ends.
Now you flower, and you're fully grown,
In reality, you're not alone.

It's crucial to grasp a home,
Adventure into a world full of the unknown.
Your heart isn't heavy, and your soul isn't so blue,
So you found your escape,
Feel not an ounce of rue.

Rhian Reeks (15)
Caldicot School, Caldicot

I'm Fine

I would say I'm fine,
Even though it would be a lie,
Actually, I wasn't fine,
Because I had something on my mind.

It would cause my palms to sweat,
My face to look full of dread,
My ears to be ringing,
My head to be spinning,
My heart to be racing,
And my legs to be shaking.

This can happen to anyone,
And it's certainly not fun,
So if you're like me,
And have anxiety,
Know you're not the only one,
And there's no need to run,
So when someone asks what's on your mind,
Don't put on a smile and say you're fine,
Tell them how you feel,
And make sure to be real,
Maybe they can help,
On how you have felt,
And remember even if you don't believe it,
Everything will get better, bit by bit.

Emily Luke (13)
Caldicot School, Caldicot

Untitled

Ba dum. Ba dum. Ba dum.

My heart speeds, I buffer,
Just carry on, ignore it,
It's tough but I'm tougher.

Ba dum. Ba dum. Ba dum.

My legs, anticipating, light up in pain,
Each step twists and turns my ankles,
And as I stand, I feel the weight of my brain.

Ba dum. Ba dum. Ba dum.

The doctors reassured me,
They said it was nothing, so I ignored it,
Standing tall as a tree.

Ba dum. Ba dum. Ba dum.

My vision fills with blacks and whites,
An angelic view as I plunge to the floor.
What a plight.

Ba dum. Ba dum. Ba dum.

My thoughts depart from my head,
Except for one shining through the fog,
I know I'll wake up later, tired, feeling dread,
So in all truth, I missed my bed.

Ba dum. Ba dum.

Nye Thomas (16)
Caldicot School, Caldicot

Live Life To The Fullest

Living life by a schedule
Is like living life bound by chains
Live your life not confined by lists and rules
Get adrenaline into your brain.

Get out into the world, explore yourself
Fly a super-speed plane or train your big brilliant brain
Find the real you, not someone else from a book on a shelf
Or a figure from a campaign.

Be unique, try some interests
Cosplay, sports, or anything else
Do what you think fits you best
Try something even if it puts you on ice.

Find all the things that you love and travel the world
Find those things and keep them even through an exodus
Break people's expectations and let your path unfurl
Don't be scared, you have friends and family to help you.

Elliott Bevan (9)
Caldicot School, Caldicot

The Book That Sets Us Free

When busy days I want to lay
And stay till night turns to day
Just me, wasting away.

This is when I pick up a book
Cosy in a little nook.

Through pages that flutter like butterflies
We chase the sun where the horizon lies
An escape from the hum of the everyday
In the land of our dreams, we frolic and play.

For those who cannot speak, get a voice
For those who cannot vote, get a choice
Without it, my head feels like a banging drum
Which even though I try so hard I can never outrun.

For it helps me ease the peace
And helps me smooth the crease.

Me and you are not the same
A book for you is a different game.

Jess Bartlett (13)
Caldicot School, Caldicot

Put On A Smile

Your life's a journey, not a game,
Some days are good, while others are bad.
The ones we meet are nearly the same,
With many happy, others miserable.

We're here on Earth to learn daily,
To treat each day with hope and grace,
And show sympathy in return,
To many on life's road we face.

Embrace each day with maximum love,
Because our days on Earth are few.
Make friends with people, make them feel your love,
In what you say and do.

Laughter is like a needed kiss,
Travelling onward, day by day.
It will bring about joy and bliss,
Be kind and give that smile away.

Kaitlyn Williams (13)
Caldicot School, Caldicot

Wise To Weak

How strange a soul could alter,
After a neglectful time.
As an individual grows older,
Somewhat loses their wits and wise.

Lavished upon tuition,
Simply to discard their own ambition.
Immensity gifted, yet drained,
Crushing weight towards an idle brain.

Canny and cunning,
Falls to drowsy and sluggish.
Who allows the finest at school,
Decline to spiritless and rude?

How can skills shift, in a brief course of time?
Beginning from scripts and scholarships,
Until socials and screen time.
So lively in passion,
Switches to lifeless in emotion.

Maddie Williams (13)
Caldicot School, Caldicot

Streets On The Edge

A needless situation,
Just a wrong look given,
An argument starts,
Then a glimpse of steel.

A swift lunge forward,
With a thrust of anger,
The shocked boy falls,
From the pain and fear.

The crowds gather round,
As the gang retreat.
They did all they could,
It was just too late.

In one crazy moment,
Everything changed,
Another life taken,
Two futures slain.

As the news sadly tells,
"It's happened again,"
This has to stop,
Things have to change.

Ania Heales (13)
Caldicot School, Caldicot

Body Dysmorphia

Body dysmorphia
A stab, a blade, a killer of pride
Away from the mirror is where I hide.

My love for food is not enough
Quick! Put it away, you're eating too much
Starve, starve, starve, don't eat
Without the perfect body, I am not complete.

But away I go from the mirror
Escaping the shadows, I can find my way
No longer bound by a heavy chain
Focusing on talents
Focusing on dreams
I won't let my body determine what I mean.

Maryam Rishi (13)
Caldicot School, Caldicot

Emotions

Emotions are complex, hard to explain.
Emotions are difficult, like a scribble inside the brain.

Sometimes they're easy, and quick to pinpoint.
But sometimes they're tough, like I'm held at gunpoint.

They're hard to understand, but easy to cover.
With a mask of happiness, touch to discover.

Beneath the mask, the tears well up in my eyes.
But I hold them back, so as not to disturb my disguise.

Talia Brigden (13)
Caldicot School, Caldicot

Untitled

Rain is cold
Rain is wet
Storms are loud
Rain pours heavily
Storms are loud, why?
Is that how they scream?
To let the anger out and be free?
Rain is the sky crying
Because it needs to let it out.
You step outside
You smell the air, it's fresh and refreshing
You can smell the damp grass and the fresh pavement.
It's almost peaceful.
A glimpse of freedom.

Callie Sedlen (9)
Caldicot School, Caldicot

For Love Is Your Sin

The dove calls upon you tonight
Or was it the crow that bemoaned murder?
Where here lay your knight, slain
By tongues that loathed against;
Incinerated despair and annihilating pain
And the moulding of mistranslations
From the static communication in-between.

Thirst and hunger slithered in all,
Were only some tempted by the serpent?
Desires that differed became your fall;
Repent it with your soul, chastise your heart
For nothing else can sacrifice your part
Of a grasp for an ever-longing affection.
A litany of keepsakes erased and gone
With societal shuns, with everything done;
Your selfsame stares, your hidden affairs
And with all of them unaware, unable to care.

Bathed in the pale moonlight
Unwillingly dragged to the centre of sight
Of a society's epiphany, something uncanny
Arisen within their minds, disgusted by the kind.
Forever tugging your deceit along
Yet nothing is left to do but;
Beg as your final amendment,

Set fire to letters left unsent,
Too late to ever repent!

Isolated beneath your sorrow
Has your breathing gone hollow,
Has your blood begun to shed?
Apologies and resentment for how you led,
Of how simultaneously we were dead.
One deed, two bodies, and the callous crowd -
The ones to tell what's not allowed
Eradicate those who went against
And those who never could repent;
"They sold their souls," is what they sensed,
All due to their love being taken for sin.

Kai Bennett (16)
Carrickfergus Grammar School, Carrickfergus

The Big Apple

The Big Apple, the American dream
The city that never sleeps
As I gaze outward towards the shrunken sunrise
Overpowered by the stench of an LED-lit fog
I ponder this path, the city rat's way of life
From Manhattan to Queens to Coney Island
All I see is the big-screen cityscape
A never-ending abyss of telemarketing and designer labels
Through smoke-stained subway station glass, looming skyscrapers tear through the blue sky
Polluting it with angry fumes of black and white
Painting clean air with a monochrome watercolour wash
Screens plaster the world around as any skyline fails to be seen
I've seen this place before
I swear I know this place, this path, that stop, the city rat's way of life
It all seems so familiar like I've been walking these roads for years
Fifth Avenue, West Side, Broadway Ave
It all feels too real, yet somehow all too fake
An artificial world, a city within a city, and an American dream.

Niamh McKinney (16)
Carrickfergus Grammar School, Carrickfergus

The Forest Escape

Escape to me is the forest breeze
A little bird flits down from the trees
The light blue sky of spring settles in
Nature's first green is bold to the brim

Tall stems streaked with amber bright
I wander through the woods in delight
The sway of the branches
The whistling of the wind
Pines bearded in moss
In the mid-wood's brim

Away from the city's roaring fuss
In the forest dark and hush
Where birds sing and squirrels climb
This place is so divine
It is this place that beckons me
For this is what escape means to me.

Matthew Clarke (15)
Carrickfergus Grammar School, Carrickfergus

A World Yet To Set Free

Oh people we know you are scared,
But soon one day you will be set free.
The lives of innocent people dying will soon end and joy will dazzle around until the days end.

No colour of skin should ever divide,
As we bleed and we may stand with pride.
No faith, no gender, no way we pray,
Should make us targets for haters' decay.

Many lands destroyed due to war,
With all children's hopes and dreams disappearing to the unknown.
Give us a reason why we should fight, why must we kill,
When peace is around us, nowhere to go.

Stop the fear, stop the lies,
Stop the pain in the innocents' eyes.
Stop the bullying, stop the blame,
No human should ever live in pain.

The world to share, a home to each and every one,
No wall too high, no heart too small.
Oh people we know you are scared,
But one day you will be set free.

Zulekha Farzand Ali (11)
Copley Academy, Stalybridge

It Was Once Their Cruel Ways

In a school a girl lived in shadowy days,
Her spirit dimmed by the taunts and cruel ways,
Each morning brought stares cold and hard,
Leaving her in sadness and deeply scarred.

One day, on one gloomy walk home,
She stumbled across a ball, so weird and unknown.
As she walked to the ball with great confusion,
There became her greatest illusion.

She kicked the ball, all anger in her feet,
She felt as if no longer in defeat.
The ball had so much power,
It could have rolled for another hour.

A blow of a whistle, a signal to run,
She outran the shadows as victory begun.
With a smile on her face and a ball by her side,
Her spirit was finally opened wide.

Nevaeh Norton (11)
Copley Academy, Stalybridge

Me And The Stage

I check my costume, my make-up, my hair,
I'm ready to go,
Deep breath in,
Deep breath out,
I walk onstage,
The bright light's shining in my face,
Everyone's looking at me,
Good, I want them to,
I take a deep breath and open my mouth to sing,
This is where I want to be,
On the stage, singing my heart out,
Here, I don't have to be Nell,
I don't have to be the 'quiet' girl,
The nerd, the shy, the weird girl,
Here, I can escape from all that and be...
The 'wow, she's great!' girl and the,
'She was such a good singer!' girl,
I hold the last note, and the applause sweeps me away,
This is where I want to be.

Nell Swettenham (12)
Copley Academy, Stalybridge

The Harsh Reality Escape

Some people may think that the only way to escape from
life is through the internet or their phone, or in their bed,
where they burrow their minds and sorrow,
but I say otherwise, there's more to life than beds and phones,
you have family and friends who can help you when you're feeling low.

But there's still more than that,
there's your loved ones and friends
and adventure and joy that you still have time to get.

And then there is the negative,
the bad things that flow,
like insults and fear,
but there's no need to be scared or to scurry in fear,
you have friends and family
who always have your back when most needed.

Archie Curtis-Bailey (14)
Copley Academy, Stalybridge

Searching For Peace

I look around, life spins in a ring,
A cycle of tasks that routine does bring.
We call it duty, a weight we bear,
But after long days, I'm left in despair.

With many friends, yet I feel alone,
In places, my heart turns into stone.
No one reaches out,
Neither do I dare.

I hear the cries of pain and strife,
Of unfairness cutting like a knife.
Yet we stay silent,
Peace feels hard to find here.

I dream for skies, with colours so bright,
No phones, no messages, just calm and light.
A place to rest, where I can be free,
A world of peace, just waiting for me.

Saanvi Deshbhratar (13)
Copley Academy, Stalybridge

Truly Free

I look around, left and right, there's no one there.
It gives me thoughts that I cannot bear.
That I'm alone.
Until I find people who are similar to me.
They like me for being me
And then I begin to feel truly free.
My friends are there for me, and for them, it is I.
But sometimes I still feel alone, mentally, not physically.
So then I try my hobbies, to see if they can help me.
I strum my brown acoustic on which I used to say:
I cannot do this.
But I cleared my head of those thoughts
I broke the chain.
Now ask yourself, *am I truly free?*

Lily Murphy (12)
Copley Academy, Stalybridge

Things I Want To Do

I want to escape from life,
Even though it was given by God,
It makes me feel odd.

I want to escape from friends,
The ones that should never end,
They can make you sad and mad and grey,
But also happy.

I should run away from racism,
It's unjust and evil, it is cruel and not fair.
If it were me, I would escape to my home which is my very own,
It makes me feel safe as if I were in space.
While in there, I reflect on my day, whether it was bad or sad,
I wish it would go away,
All I ever want is to escape.

Keane Ashton (14)
Copley Academy, Stalybridge

The Dream

Mental health can be a tricky thing to escape
What is this place?
I go to school, I hate it there
When it all kicks in, it really is a scare
My stomach feels like a knot
I just want it to stop
I look in the mirror, thinking, *why do I have to stay?*
Can't you go away?
I go to sleep dreaming of a place
Where all the bad thoughts get lost without a trace
Everything's amazing, where there's not a single worry
But all of a sudden, everything starts to scurry
I wake up, I'm back here again...

Darcy Gooch (11)
Copley Academy, Stalybridge

Overlooked Words

Mental health.
Nobody understands the day-to-day struggles that go on beneath the surface.
The surface that's all happy and bubbly is also drained, depressed and debating life.
Just like an iceberg showing only parts of the picture.
Everything I felt yesterday feels completely different today.
All I want is an escape.
To feel free of my struggles.
To live my life like all of my friends.
To live without questioning my existence.
To escape the war going on inside my mind.

Imogen McBurnie (14)
Copley Academy, Stalybridge

Remember

R emember all of the people who lost their lives during World War I and II
E very family and every person was affected by war
M emories from war are everlasting
E veryone marching across the muddy trenches drowned in blood
M any people sacrificed themselves to save their country
B ritain needed allies to win the war
E nemies attacking one another
R emember the soldiers couldn't escape from the nightmare they were trapped in.

Jess Clegg (13)
Copley Academy, Stalybridge

An Ideal World

There should be a world for everyone
A world with harmony
A world where everywhere is peaceful
A world where no one collides and events don't end in conflict
A world where people are not discrimated against because of who they are
A world where everyone has their own personality and uniqueness
A world where money doesn't matter
Maybe even a different planet
A world where poverty is not a thing
A world with no conflict

An ideal world.

Max Van Massey (12)
Copley Academy, Stalybridge

Untitled

There are many things going on around the world, like war and bullying.
There are many things going on, and many people may be very sad because they've lost their families.

If you walk around the place and count to ten you can calm down.
If that doesn't work, there are many things you can do,
Like breathe and think of a calm place where there are clouds
Or somewhere you like which can calm you down.
If you think more about calm stuff you will get there.

Jan Judzewicz (11)
Copley Academy, Stalybridge

A Quiet Town

All is quiet in the Quiet Town but soon that might not last for long,
You notice bombs are dropped on the Quiet Town,
You rush to safety quicker than ever,
The said-to-be Quiet Town now lies in blood and rubble,
You flee to the coast, where boats await you,
Waiting patiently for your turn to go,
You get called down and feel nervous, praying nothing bad happens,
Rumours you've heard of boats capsizing,
Soon you are sailing away from the Quiet Town.

Toby McLaren (12)
Copley Academy, Stalybridge

Raging Reality Running Riot

You're all grown up,
going to high school.
Your parents give you a spare phone
so if you need to you can ring your parents.
But now you can't get off of it,
your head is glued to it,
trying to escape reality by locking yourself in your room on social media.
You want to escape but the reality is you have nothing else to do.
Your mind is dragged away from the expectations
and all you want is to fit in,
but your phone took that away.

Freya Neville-Cooper (13)
Copley Academy, Stalybridge

Escape The World Around Me

If I close my eyes for a second
I can escape from the world around me
The world that once was a calm and peaceful place to be
Which is now loud and scary
I wish I could escape from this war to my imaginary land
Filled with the things I love and enjoy
But I can't, it doesn't feel right anymore
All I hear around me, around my country
Is screaming, gunshots
If I close my eyes for a second,
I can escape from the world around me.

Phoebie Ryan (11)
Copley Academy, Stalybridge

Strangers

In life there are strangers
Here, there and, well, everywhere
But most of the time we don't pay attention to that random person who held the door open that one time,
Or when they compliment your clothes, hair, nails, and even your make-up,
I guess what I'm trying to say is don't just walk by...
Say thank you and maybe next time you could give a stranger a compliment.

Jessica Vickers (11)
Copley Academy, Stalybridge

Escape

The stark reality is the transition from years 6-7.
My mind explodes with thoughts.
Can I settle in?
My sweet escape, football, let's score a goal to settle the thoughts.

Marching from class to class,
School to school,
Rather stay in one classroom.

Like English, maths and science are not enough,
History, geography and languages open the door.

Raja Akram (12)
Copley Academy, Stalybridge

Global Warming Is A No!

Animals and nature matter
When I see how it affects them it makes my heart shatter
Our world shouldn't be like this
It's turning into the abyss
Glass and rubbish on our beaches
Animals covered in leeches
It's extremely unfair
People have no heart to spare
Think about the person you could be
If you helped to keep our Earth clean.

Charlotte Leeming (12)
Copley Academy, Stalybridge

Home

We all love being home,
But sometimes want to escape.
We run around, but when we're stressed, we escape.
In your imagination, you can be dancing on a cloud, singing on a stage,
All your wildest dreams can come true.
No matter when you want or need to escape,
Home is where you are.

Elsie Foley-Turner (12)
Copley Academy, Stalybridge

Set Free

The world today
Isn't the same as yesterday.
The world now
Shouldn't take a bow
The world today is full of regret
As every day you are a threat
You should be you and not the
Person you are standing next to
So set your wings free
And be who you want to be.

Isabella Lockwood (14)
Copley Academy, Stalybridge

Help With Stress

Do you ever feel stressed?
Like you feel like a balloon that's about to pop?
Well, to help with that here is some advice.
You could try being with your friends or spending time with family.
Or maybe going on a nice holiday somewhere.
But there is much more!

Lewis Blenkinsop (13)
Copley Academy, Stalybridge

The Flooding Heart

Please, please tell me,
What's wrong with the society we live in?
Where people are judged,
By their skin tone, race,
And even gender,
Where people actually
just want to end their life.

Think about people,
Who are being treated like this,
Their minds filled with questions
about why they were born like this.
Their hearts filled with sorrow,
Their ears filled with people
saying bad things about them.
Their mouths filled with the words
"I am so sorry for being born like this."

They even get to the point,
Where they decide
to end their own life.
Where is the justice?
Why can't the world be fair to everyone?
So let's all join together
to destroy racism and bullying.

Deona Jaison (13)
Dedworth Middle School, Windsor

My ADHD

As I walk through the gates, I wish I could turn back.
I know it's going to be another day, where I fail and forget.
I see my friends, they are laughing and playing.
I walk over, jumping and shouting.
The bell rings, I dread what comes.
I am told I have too much energy.
The teachers cannot handle me.
First period comes, I look at my seat and picture all of the ways I will embarrass myself.
The teachers ask me questions and I am under pressure.
I forget stuff and lose my focus.
As I look at the board, I am reading words, but my mind is in a completely different place.
I get frustrated easily, and I stare at a blank page.
It is now the shift between lessons.
That one small movement break between the hours of stillness.
The hallways are loud and energetic, with people pushing and shoving.
My energy bursts and I can't help but smile.
I shout, I push and excitedly dart to my next lesson.
As soon as I open the classroom door, my eyes feel heavy and my excitement fades.
It is time for maths now.
When the bell rings for break, I feel glad that I can let loose.
I stand in the queue in the canteen, impatiently waiting for the mozzarella sticks.

When I reach the Astroturf, I throw my bag to the side and run for the goal.
As I am having fun, I hear the same bell. Fun's over.
I realise I am going back to my seat.
It's now fourth period and I can't stop moving.
I stare out of the window, distracted by the birds.
The teacher calls my name and I snap back to reality, science equations on the board.
She looks at me as if I am silly and I hear sniggers all over.
My cheeks go red, and my words get jumbled.
She rolls her eyes and sighs an exaggerated breath.
It's at moments like this where I wish I would disappear.
Time for the next lesson.
I turn to my friend and ask, "What do we have next?"
Food tech, I grin like a pumpkin on Halloween night.
My favourite lesson at last.
We are cooking pasta.
I chop, peel and dice... the final result looks like heaven.
The final bell rings in my ears.
I walk back through the same gate, with my group of friends.
I realise that sometimes things can be bad, but that makes the good things better.
I made it through the day, no negative behaviour points today.

Callum O'Connor (12)
Dedworth Middle School, Windsor

A Poem About Bullying

We arrive at school, gates so tall, where the bullies seem to know it all,
As we sit in the science block, the bullies start to mock,
Like the clock going tick-tock,
Off to the first lesson where the bullies still won't listen,
As a tear rolls down, it starts to glisten,
Off to another lesson where the bullies continue to threaten,
Now to break time when the bullies make a hate crime,
We skip and run, but the bullies are still no fun,
At lunch, they start to taunt,
And I know this will later haunt,
Off to the last lesson of the day,
To hear yet more of what they have to say,
Now it's the end of the day,
And I'd like to say, hooray,
But it's just another day,
Of my smiles that have gone away.

Kaycee Ireland (13)
Dedworth Middle School, Windsor

Escaping Reality

Escaping reality is a hard thing to do
Especially when reality is keeping you
Holding you back from having a dream
Dreaming of a sunny beach
Or snow on a winter's morning

Maybe it's a magical candy forest
With an all-you-can-eat buffet

A dream that helps you forget about your miserable day
In the class being bullied because of your looks
Hearing the laughter of your classmates teasing you

Then you get into English and go sit down
All the laughter gets drowned out
Instead, it's replaced with the sound of cameras flashing
And people shouting, then you realise you're famous

Escaping reality is peaceful
When the world around you is miserable.

Grace Phipps (11)
Dedworth Middle School, Windsor

Held By Fear

I wake up with shaking thoughts,
Running through my mind.
A silent panic,
From the start.
I look for peace,
I look for light,
But the shaking thoughts,
Are holding me tight.

I try to stay calm,
To keep my peace,
But in my mind,
I'm still not at ease.
I breathe in deep,
But can't escape,
These fears.

I drown in panic and dismay,
It creates clouds of fear,
My mind is unclear.
I'm lost in deep thoughts,
I'm scared to face these fears.
I stay calm,
I try to breathe,
To take over these feelings,
Of being overtaken by anxiety.

I'm lost and panicked,
Can't explain,
These bubbles of panic.

Adan Maki (11)
Dedworth Middle School, Windsor

The Kids In Blue

I walk through the gate with a weight on my shoulders
Hoping today will just be over.

I paint a smile on my face
So nobody will know why I hate this place.

The hums of the whispers meet my ears
As a couple of kids in blue become my worst fears.

My heart begins to race, my palms begin to sweat
As their blue meets with mine, causing my spine to tremble
Not knowing what they have in mind.

I'm numb on the outside
On the inside, I'm hollow
As the kids in blue make me fear my own shadow.

I finally think I've escaped
But the blue grab at me
Causing me to think I don't matter...

Ruby Lock (13)
Dedworth Middle School, Windsor

Escape From School

I know what you're thinking when I say,
Escaping from school.
But trust me when I say,
Escaping is not cool.

First, you get into trouble,
Doesn't matter if you did it or not.
We all have that one person,
Who escaped school a lot.

Second, after that has happened,
You probably get caught.
So all that work, all those miles,
You've fought...

Just to go back where you started.
So even if you think you're smart,
Just know that you've been outsmarted.

Freedom's taste is bittersweet.
In shadows of the lessons lost,
I find the weight of what I see,
And count the heavy cost.

Dylan Turner (12)
Dedworth Middle School, Windsor

Reality

Upon a soul,
Upon a mind
Sat a child
Like no other kind,
Mind like no other,
His brother watching over,
Creating a place
For his sibling
To have some space
That he deserved,
To have some time preserved,
Just to escape reality,
That would make him feel
Like he had some speciality,
That he forever needed
Just to be ignored,
Something that he
Would adore
Is to be loved even more,
And there is something
That he needs even more,
It is to escape
From this godforsaken place
That sits in one's mind.

Dexter Bull (12)
Dedworth Middle School, Windsor

The Locked Door That Never Worked

Do you like locked doors?
It looks like the law,
The people don't like it,
It looks like feet,
It never worked,
The door was shut,
Forever and ever,
It is the worst thing you have ever seen,
It looks like an egg,
The people ran away,
Looking at the locked door,
Feeling like a dog paw,
All night, the door didn't work,
Looking like people saying, "Jerk,"
It has a lot of angry faces,
Looking like a tooth had been taken out,
So don't come near the locked door,
Otherwise, you are over the law.

Harley Brant (12)
Dedworth Middle School, Windsor

Why?

Why do they stare, why do they judge?
Why do they whisper, why do they nudge?
Skin's just skin, it doesn't define, so why
Do they act like theirs is divine?

They say we're different, but we're the same.
Yet still, they call me hurtful names.
They turn their backs, they shut me out,
As if they know what I'm about.

But no more silence, no more shame,
I won't let their words decide,
Who I am, or what's inside.
We all have a worth, we all have a pride,
No hate can crush the inside.

Zoha Chaudhary (12)
Dedworth Middle School, Windsor

Racism

What I am about to talk about is not new to you
What if you are the one who is racist to pupils?
Just put yourself in their shoes
You wouldn't like it if anyone was bullying you about your culture, skin tone or religion
Non-stop, every night, hoping the next day someone will apologise for their action
Them crying themselves to sleep
Taking all the anger, all the hate to someone online.
If we stop it all, no one would start hating themselves
Everyone would be blissful
No one would hate themself or even cry themself to sleep.

Gunn Walia (12)
Dedworth Middle School, Windsor

My Sorrows

Once, I was sad and alone in my pain
My wave of sadness and sorrow
No one could help me, not even a pea
But this is how I recharge my energy

Abuse is what I find sickening
Once, I was being tortured day and night
It made me sad
But that's when I became bad

The touch was like nails on your skin
Taste was like vomit
Smell was like a cloud of cigarettes that never ended
What I heard was unspeakable
All I could see was blood and gore.

Lucy Martin (11)
Dedworth Middle School, Windsor

The Life Of School

School. Everyone might hate it
But you don't know the fun behind it
English, you might think it is a waste of time
Maths, well, you know the drill
But everyone loves art
Because it makes you an artist
In food tech, the food that is harvest
Turns into a scrumptious meal
But in PE you are a champion
School is full of bullies and ups and downs
You should enjoy school
Because you never know who you will
Be in the future.

Roxi Hasley (12)
Dedworth Middle School, Windsor

There Goes Gravity

Your mind will start to flow a river of thoughts
So you just need to escape reality
Oh! There goes gravity...
I just escaped reality.

Some people ask how it feels
But first, you need desire and to believe in yourself
Lose yourself in the music, in the moment
You know you want it!

Thoughts are piling over each other
Faster than the speed of light
Now overflowing, I can't focus on life
I must escape reality.

Govind Singh Sehra (12)
Dedworth Middle School, Windsor

Retreat To Dreamland

Retreat to Dreamland
To escape the horrid Human Land
Poison, war, and global warming all
Happiness in Humanland
But not in Dreamland.

Dreamland is happy
No dying, poison, war or
Global warming here in
My Dreamland.

When I'm back at Human Land
It's stressful and hard
But when I return to
Dreamland I'm happy and joyful
Once again.

Jessica Clark (11)
Dedworth Middle School, Windsor

Loop

Let me escape this loop
It's all I ever do.
Wake up, go to school, sleep
Let me escape this loop.

Let me escape this loop
Nothing new on my 'to-do'
Same hobbies, same people, same games.
Let me escape this loop.

Let me escape this loop
I need something better to do
It's the same thing every day
Let me escape this loop.

Amber Agacy (11)
Dedworth Middle School, Windsor

The Foolish Scientist

The eerie lab room started to shake,
A new creation began to awake,
No one could hear a sound,
Nor were they to be found,
The creation broke out, free at last,
And made an exit with a blast,
Heading towards the bustling city,
The scientist sat in pity,
What a bad day, he thought,
But he did not care,
And made something extremely rare!

Desiree Lawson (12)
Dedworth Middle School, Windsor

Flashback

A loud noise
A bang
A flash
And now it's the past
I cling to my mother
This time it may be my last.

A plane soars by
A shout
A scream
These are bad times for all
Including me.

It all goes to a blur
I'm back to the present
It all went fast
These memories are sure to last.

Rron Mulolli (12)
Dedworth Middle School, Windsor

Why?

People were residing in the building which stood firm
Only to have its time shortened in an instant
Fire envelops the haven for some people
Only wanting to flee from life's torture
The minds of refugees overflow with uncontrollable fear
Staring at the heat and hearing noises that are imposing
Whistling sounds into their ears
"Why?" they question, as the reason seems rather nefarious
"Why?" they question, as the hordes of people flood the roads in front
Social media posts influence such violent behaviour
The idea seems so idiotic to do so
The level of these follow-the-leader games seems incomprehensible as they march to their destination
Whilst the actions of these rioters become nonsensical
Overflowing like herds of animals occurs with the aim of eradication
Which is seen to be something that is judicious in the eyes of some
"Why?" they question, as to why these refugees have the right to be here
"Why?" they question, as to why enforcement forbids the escape of these infiltrators from this life to the next.

Cameron Birchill (16)
Denstone College, Denstone

The Pages Call

The clock ticks loudly, each beat a sigh
A heavy hush, beneath the sky
The morning's grey, the lessons drag
A lifeless sense, my spirits sag

The desks feel cold, the walls close in
The air is stale, no spark within
Each voice and echo, each step a weight
An endless march in a dreary state

But crack the spine, and time takes flight
The world ignites with colours bright
A wizard's spell, a villain's plot
A thousand worlds I'd once forgot

The building hums with hidden lore
Each tree conceals a hidden door
The teacher's words, a lowly muffle
Deafened by my hero's tussle

Through open books I leap, I soar
The mundane fades, I'm bound no more
When life feels stuck, the pages call
Imagination beats it all.

William Kelly (13)
Denstone College, Denstone

Untitled

Poems can free the mind,
Poems can challenge your imagination,
Writing can take you to a place,
A place of freedom and no hate,

Reading can let your mind run free
And let you escape from reality,
Illustrating can let your mind flow,
All ideas can be revealed.

Tons of people listening,
Waiting for brilliant ideas to come alive,
Making the world a better place
Minutes at a time.

Get your ideas heard,
Let your creativity run wild
And let your dreams come true.

Izzy Houghton (12)
Denstone College, Denstone

Hidden

Hidden out of sight,
Hidden in the air,
There's a little piece of magic,
That's hidden everywhere.

You may never find it,
This magic in the air,
But never stop believing,
It's hidden everywhere.

If you keep on hunting,
For this magic in the air,
You're sure to, one day, find it,
For it's hidden everywhere.

And once it's in your grasp,
This magic in the air,
It's with you all the time,
For it's hidden everywhere.

Never stop believing,
In this magic in the air,
Although it's hard to see it,
It's hidden everywhere.

Hidden out of sight,
Hidden in the air,
There's a little piece of magic,
That's hidden everywhere.

Felicity Baker (12)
Denstone College, Denstone

Cricket Rules

C alling for a wicket,
R unning to field a ball,
I n the batter's head,
C utting it for four
K nuckle balls being bowled,
E conomy rate is creeping up,
T he run chase is on.

R uns being scored everywhere,
U nder edge, caught by the keeper,
L ap sweep for six,
E nergetic running every ball,
S tumped. The last wicket has gone.

Aidan Jones (12)
Denstone College, Denstone

Death And Destruction

The knife's cold touch
My heart's slowing beat
The murderous feeling
As I become mincemeat

The bugs in my eyes
The mud on my feet
My bones coming free
And death as I sleep

I feel Lucifer's cold grip
And fall down underneath

Bear Yates (14)
Denstone College, Denstone

Fragments Of Pretend

You looked around on Monday,
At wonders of the world.
But dig a little deeper,
And wings of smoke unfurl.

On the shallow surface,
All is calm and still.
But dig a little deeper,
You're alone up on a hill.

Looking down around you,
Others passing by.
But dig a little deeper,
And you can see them cry.

You look around on Monday,
And start to see the truth.
The peaceful world is just pretend,
You find the bitter proof.

Isla Soper (14)
Devonport High School For Girls, Peverell

What It Means To Be A Benjamin

B rave, being a Benjamin is something I'm proud of, you're born strong, live strong and die strong.
E verlasting love, Benjamins love every living thing.
N ever-ending passion, we stand up for what we believe in.
J oyful, we are always looking on the bright side.
A ctive, we are strong and active, it is in our blood.
M ind, we can escape reality with our mind.
I magination, we are very imaginative.
N ever regret anything, YOLO!

Naomi Benjamin (11)
Gowerton School, Gowerton

The Boring Poem

It is a feeling worse than sorrow,
Something which one cannot borrow,
The stress it causes me doesn't change,
For once, this feels strange,
To forever never change,
I am a star in a galaxy that does not move,
And there is nothing here to choose,
But my brightness I will not lose,
Even when no atoms are there to fuse,
Boredom is a pain,
It is a chain,
From which I have nothing to gain.

Pedro Goncalves Gurgel Filho (14)
Kingsbury High School, Kingsbury

The Place Behind Closed Doors

What do I feel trapped by?
What ifs and closed doors?
Or cracking pressure and open floors?
Yes, the floors are yours to share your voice.
No need to hide away; make the right choice.
Stand up and speak out.
Why escape to a place that's not so loud?
Prying eyes that seem to stare.
Are always there;
To haunt you. Taunt you.
Make a fool of you.
It's just some eyes.
No need to hide.
No need to run and run and cry.

Escape.
What a lovely word.
Used to bring hope as a noun.
But strike fear as a verb.
Why are you running?
What led you down this path?
What will meet you in the dark?
Is it the fear of what could, should, would be?
Is it a lightless room, locked, with a thrown-away key?
Is it the harsh-handed shove that you have to be better?

Or is it the crowding eyes that make a space,
That. Much. Smaller.

My escape comes with the rush of waves.
The scent of salted spray, my protecting mist.
My peace comes with what Poseidon creates.
The fresh joy water brings is the anticipation
Of an unopened gift.

My escape is found in the placing of a page.
The reading of well - wondered words.
The smell of wisdom is unlimited by age.
With the scratch of a pen.
And the eye of wonderful sight.
My escape is the places.
That I have come to read and write.

Issie Williams (13)
Langley Park School For Girls, Beckenham

The Endless Run

In the distant horizon
A glistening rainbow shines
It's peaceful glare beckons me
So I dazedly stand up and begin walking towards it
Getting more desperate to reach it, my slow stride forms into a trot
Every time I think about reaching the rainbow, it makes me want to reach it sooner
Before I know it, I am sprinting across the fields of darkness
My cold feet can feel the mud below
I go even faster now, sweat streaming off my face like waterfalls
But there's no hope
No matter how hard I try, the rainbow just gets further
Further and further away
This isn't about reaching a rainbow
It's about reaching peace.

Florence Sanders (11)
Sheringham High School, Sheringham

I Don't Want To Be Here

Scream, shout, crash, and bang
The world is against me without a doubt
Quietly sneaking out the window
Don't Disturb hangs on my door
I sneak out, it's kind of a bore
Tipsy people regretting every second
Flashing car lights going flicker, flicker
Wanting to go back but it's too late now
The sun peeks out of the clouds
Relief going through my bones
Seeing the news, tears fill my eyes
Noticing my old cracked door
My face is getting wet
And hearing the concerned words we missed
You made the world get off my back
And for once in my life I feel wanted.

Evie Furze (11)
Sheringham High School, Sheringham

Your Pale Blue Eyes

Let me look into your pale blue eyes,
I will see what you refuse to say.
Your secrets mean no harm to me,
For I carry my own dissarray.

In your silence, I find solace.
A pain that mirrors mine,
And though you hide, I understand,
The weight of what's confined.

Like the sea your eyes shine,
A glimpse of what once was mine,
We seek escape,
Where past and pain subside.
But even as I drift away,
Those eyes will beg for me to stay.

For you hide no shame, cast me away,
But I will forever have an ethereal shine,
On your pale blue eyes.

Brieanna Baldwin (12)
Sheringham High School, Sheringham

School

As you walk to the class,
The bell ringing in your ear,
The fear of being late,
It's like the teachers decide your fate.

As you sit in a class
And the teacher talks,
You slowly turn to the clock.
Oh, time goes so slow with Miss Willow!

When in the line for lunch,
Oh, what fun!
All that's left is an old bun.
You sit and eat in a rush, then quickly jump to your feet

Last lesson of the day,
Oh hooray!
Science, oh what a breeze!
As the day may have to end,
The rush, oh the rush at the end of the day.

Mabel-Faith Smith
Sheringham High School, Sheringham

Bullied And Broken

There goes an alert,
Someone is hurt,
They were hit in the face, such a disgrace,
As their heart begins to race.
It's not fair,
But the bully doesn't seem to care,
Just why is there a fight? It's just not right.
Words after words,
And being called nerds,
Why did you purposely hurt someone's joint, what is the point?
Oh dear, oh dear,
Sadly, someone just shed a tear.
Why aren't they having fun?
Why aren't they running into the hot, red sun?
Treat people the way you want to be treated.

Ava Mai Mardell (12)
Sheringham High School, Sheringham

Untitled

In the mirrored halls of youth, she walks,
A shadow in sunlight stitched with scars,
The laughter of friends, a faded whisper,
Echoes of a dad lost in his drink.
She can still taste the anger,
Bitter like the last drop of whisky,
The crash of fists and dreams shattered,
A storm that raged in their small, cramped room.
"Why?" she asked the stars, hoping they could hold her question,
"Why did love bend into a fist?
Why did care hide behind a bottle?"

Nicole Boswell (12)
Sheringham High School, Sheringham

Anxiety

Anxiety is a horrible thing,
Sometimes it takes control.
It makes us feel down,
Makes us feel bad, and we frown.
Some can hide it, some cannot,
Sometimes it just creeps through.
But remember, anxiety isn't you.

It can snatch our identity,
We try to hide,
It feels like a big storm inside.
We try to act fine,
But it grows worse and makes us cry.
It's better to let it go,
Otherwise, we can feel worse.
But if you tell others, they can help,
Don't stand there keeping it to yourself.

Hannah Bennett (12)
Sheringham High School, Sheringham

The Lost Man

I lie in the rain,
Where you don't know my pain,
You assumed, you judged, that I got hooked on drugs,
You don't know the pain I'm in,
I lost my dog, I just wanted it to stop,
My family, who didn't finish happily,
I lost it all,
Including myself,
So leave, I lie in my pain,
Under the sky, I start to cry.

Reuban Bellingham (13)
Sheringham High School, Sheringham

The Boar Of War

War is an untameable boar,
A boar so vicious so vile,
As it rushes down the rapids of life,
Stabbing us with the knife,
The knife of sorrow, the knife of greed,
A greed we do not need.
We need love and let it be free,
Free as a dove,
So we can tame the boar that is war.

Jack Farmer Stowe (13)
Sheringham High School, Sheringham

Within The Worlds Of Ink

Numbers and grades define who I am,
As and percentages – my worth in their hands.
They tell me to reach for the highest of skies,
But the further I climb, the more I feel tied.

In shadows deep, where pages glow bright,
Ink spills a doorway, a world bathed in light.
No watchful eyes, no weight to bear,
No pressure, no judgment – just freedom to spare.

As the clock ticks slower, the world starts to fade,
Which book will pull me in, the next adventure to invade?
Escaping reality, I fall into the pages,
Where freedom flows like rivers, and pressure disengages.

With the turn of each page, the weight slips away,
A new tale calls, inviting me to stay.
The lands I explore breathe life into me,
And for once in my life, I am truly free.

But as the pages drift to a close, I breathe a new air,
The weight on my shoulders now easier to bear.
For the stories I've lived through aren't just for escape,
They've shaped who I am, helped me find my place.

For in the worlds of ink, I've found my peace,
Where every story helps my worries cease.
And so, though the pages may crumble with time,
The stories they've told will forever be mine.

Zainab Afsar (15)
The Fountain School, Bradford

The Elysian Fields

I opened my eyes to unravel the cheerless world ahead of me,
The dismal profiles and waspish tongues of the common herd,
Wretched and desolate faces in every direction I face,
Confusion arises, causing me to shut my eyes and shut myself from this sombre earth and rude mob...

'It's a place where everyone is kind, polite and fair
I try to smell the pure air
There is love and happiness everywhere
It's a place free from all kinds of despair
Causing me to release a sigh of bliss'.

Yet, the hell on Earth drags me back,
And wrenches my ideal world from my grasp,
All I can do is sit and stare in desolation,
In the chaotic and cluttered cosmos in my presence,
Every moment I take to return, the depravity yanks me back to reality,
Wiping out my dream,
Making every breath restricted,
Hitting me harder and making me feel diseased,
Yet I don't move an inch, and neither can I escape the nightmare.
I'm not the only one...

Munibah Khan (14)
The Fountain School, Bradford

If Dreams Stood Still

When homework stacks up and there's a pain in my head,
When the world is too loud I swoon on my bed,
My eyelids drop, my thoughts untie,
As I slip through a crack in the edge of the sky.

There's a word in my skull?

Where a swing drapes the moon and the stars are made up,
Weird? Maybe. But at least here no one shouts, "Hurry up!"
I drift to year 9, where I want school no more.
I want to sleep forever and have my energy restored.

So here I can forget the world, and blur out those crowds,
Cos my worries dissolve into cotton candy clouds,
Time doesn't tick here, it drips slow and sweet,
Like honey on toast when the flavour is peak.

But then my phone buzzes the real world appears,
A detention reminder, the sadness is clear,
But if the worries get heavy I will sleep for my sake,
And enter a paradise of heavenly escape.

Mahroosh Kashif (14)
The Fountain School, Bradford

Which Mask Should I Wear?

Which mask should I wear today?
One to fit in the world, or one to turn away?
I'm home, I'm safe, I'm free, I'm me
But outside, I must choose who I ought to be
At school I wear a mask so bright
A mask that hides my fear from sight
I'm kind, I'm soft, I won't defend
But inside I'm breaking, reaching the end

Which mask should I wear in the crowd?
The one that's quiet or the one that's loud?
I smile at those who don't deserve
I wear them all, I hide my fears, my every fall

Which mask should I wear in tomorrow's light?
The one that fits, or the one that fights?
I'm asked to shield, to hide my thoughts
Or will I ever take a break from these masks I wear?

Ieza Mohammad (15)
The Fountain School, Bradford

A Dream I Could Not Keep

I wake up in a peaceful land,
Somewhere where it's safe,
Somewhere with soft sand,
Somewhere I can escape.
I take a step and look around,
Seeing birds and tropical trees.
I hear them make a subtle sound,
This is the best place to be free.
I gently close my eyes,
Feeling the cold, gentle breeze.
As the sun begins to descend from the skies,
Hearing the splashes of the seas,
I open my eyes once more.
Sitting down and looking up at space,
As the waves hit the shore,
I think to myself, *I don't want to leave this place.*
I watch the sun set in the distance,
Feeling myself fall asleep,
Everything turning into darkness,
It was a dream I could not keep.

Ramlah Said
The Fountain School, Bradford

The Future

I stepped through time, a leap, a fall
I found myself in a different world
A metallic sky, streets so bright
I was lost! I tried to call, I whispered names
Yet no one replied.

No laughter, no joy, only metal echoes
No human voice had I heard
Except from my own, as I cried for help
Eyes once caring and warm, now ice-cold
They moved like ghosts in lifeless skin
Minds like wires, hearts like screens.

Now I knew where I was
In a future where no heart yearns
Lost in time, I tried to get back
But there was no way out.

I closed my eyes, I clenched my fists
I wished for all the past I'd lost
I knew there was no time to get back.

Sumayyah Waqas
The Fountain School, Bradford

Breaking The Cycle

Wake, school, eat, repeat,
Same dull rhyme, same old beat.
The clock hands mock, they spin, they sneer,
Trapped inside this spinning sphere.

Alarms that scream, footsteps drag,
Unfinished dreams in a heavy bag.
Pages turn but nothing's new,
The days just blur in shades of blue.

But something changes - a fire inside,
A desire to break free I cannot hide.
What if I ran, what if I crept?
Tore the script, the cycle wrecked?

No more lines, no more chains,
No more rules inside my veins.
I'll change the game, I'll break the rules,
This loop is done -
And I choose to be free.

Ilsa Khan (15)
The Fountain School, Bradford

Behind The Mask

I laugh, I joke, I play along,
Convince them that I am strong,
They see the smiles, the glee, the cheer,
But never what I truly fear.

Inside, my mind is tangled tight,
A war I fight alone at night,
Something that won't come into their sight,
They don't see that I fight.

I hide the cracks, I paint them well,
So no one sees this broken shell,
The world moves fast, I fall behind,
Lost in my mind.

So, I silence my real self and wear the mask,
Pretending is the hardest task,
And though I scream, though I fall,
No one sees me break at all.

Juwayriyah Bint-Abbas (15)
The Fountain School, Bradford

Boom!

More bombs, more lives,
Shattered dreams in flaming skies.
Hopeless hearts and teary eyes,
As terror haunts in disguise.

Children weep, mothers grieve,
Bodies lie six feet deep.
Families flee, but no place to find,
Memories hover like an eclipse in the mind.

Scars dug deep where secrets seep,
A silent cry the heart must keep.
A desperate plea,
A plan to break free.

A life full of misery and nothing but struggle,
Endless pain carved into my soul.
A destiny forged beyond our hold,
A chapter closed, a story untold.

Hafsa
The Fountain School, Bradford

Escaping From School

The room is cold
I see the sunshine dazzling outside
I can't even escape the room
The boring rules I must obey
My mind wanders
Why can't I escape the school?
I can't even see the square root of 144
That number is evil: I say, it's evil
Work and more work, there goes another dreadful day
Waiting for the day to end
It's 4pm. Thank god!
But at the end of the school day on the way home, I'll say goodbye
But remember that I'll have a bunch of homework to do at home.

Ifra Dastagir (14)
The Fountain School, Bradford

The Runaway

E agerly waiting for the teacher to turn her back
S top! I think I've just found the hack
C reak the chair to make a distracting sound
A ha! Chitter, chatter all around
P ull your coat over your head
E legantly run home and go to bed!

Naima Khan
The Fountain School, Bradford

Will They Come?

W hen they come, we're gone
 I f we even survive that long
 L onging for someone to save us
 L ife does not seem in sight

 T hat was until *he* came
 H e showed us the way
 E veryone believed we could escape
 Y elling and screaming was heard one night

 C ome and get me, run if you can
 O ne night we will be remembered
 M any of us believed; we were foolish
 E veryone knows what's happening, or at least *he* does.
   He's watching you.

Oscar Pullen (12)
Woldgate School & Sixth Form College, Pocklington

The Mansion

Underneath the moon, like a dark shadow,
The mansion towered above me, like a tall stranger.
As I stepped inside, the door made a creak.
My heart was racing, my knees felt weak.
Climbing up the rickety stairs,
I blew on the stair rail, dust filled the air.
I entered a small room, little and cosy.
There was a girl, cheeks so rosy. It couldn't be!
That was... me.

Jongpatana Saiyut (12)
Woldgate School & Sixth Form College, Pocklington

Vampires

V ampires are about,
A ware of fear and doubt.
M onsters of blood and death,
P ursuing every scent of man,
I ntent on one thing,
R eady to pounce,
E xperienced in every type of torture.
S o don't go into the woods or that will be the last of you.

Olivia Swattridge (11)
Woldgate School & Sixth Form College, Pocklington

Boy With A Toy

There was a boy
His mother got home
She gave him a toy
In fact, it was a little comb
His hair was wild
And free
But he was only a child
No harm could be
He skipped through the hallways
Hands in the air
He didn't care.

Fergus Wilson (12)
Woldgate School & Sixth Form College, Pocklington

A Good Book

R oses and daisies
E xplorers and dragons
A dventures of all sorts
D etectives with diaries
I gnorance and war
N othing better than a
G ood book.

Faye Cotton (12)
Woldgate School & Sixth Form College, Pocklington

Spring

S pring
P oppies are blooming
R ed roses too
I love spring
N ever want it to end
G o outside and enjoy nature.

Olivia Beck (11)
Woldgate School & Sixth Form College, Pocklington

The Rock

The rock on the dock
Was in shock
As he focused on the clock
With volcanic rock
The clock went *tick-tock*.

Gene Chandler (12)
Woldgate School & Sixth Form College, Pocklington

Untitled

They were all pushing me to do it
One hundred different voices screaming commands I knew I shouldn't follow
Standing at the edge of this cliff
Blood rushed through my body
Sweat dripped from my fingertips
My legs slowly collapsed in on themselves
I could hear my heartbeat in my head
I knew it would be funny for everyone watching
I knew nothing bad would happen to me if I jumped
Looking down at the still-blue water
I could see the reflection of myself telling me not to do it
The adrenaline struck my body like lightning
I leapt into the air
And for all of those ten seconds
The only thing that was lingering in my head was how people might actually like me for jumping
If I could go back to the top of that cliff
I would block everyone's voices
It's been two months since then
I'm paralysed from the neck down
I will never be normal again
The funny thing is after all of that
Not a single person knows who I am
Or what happened.

Ruby Gardner (14)
Woodbridge Park Education Services, Feltham

The Reality Of Students' Lives

School is jarring, I feel like hiding,
Grades are getting low, teens are getting high.
The twelve-year-old is pregnant and her parents wonder why.
A first-grader is swearing, a third-grader has been raped,
Just take a look around you, isn't the system just great?
Who isn't faced these days? Teens are sending nudes,
Kids are getting beaten, teachers are seeing the bruises.
No calls for help are spoken, teens are smoking weed,
Young girls are cutting, this isn't what we need.
Another kid expelled for doing a stupid dare.

Abbie Napper (15)
Woodbridge Park Education Services, Feltham

Young Writers Information

We hope you have enjoyed reading this book – and that you will continue to in the coming years.

If you're a young writer who enjoys reading and creative writing, or the parent of an enthusiastic poet or story writer, do visit our website **www.youngwriters.co.uk**. Here you will find free competitions, workshops and games, as well as recommended reads, a poetry glossary and our blog. There's lots to keep budding writers motivated to write!

If you would like to order further copies of this book, or any of our other titles, then please give us a call or visit **www.youngwriters.co.uk**.

Young Writers
Remus House
Coltsfoot Drive
Peterborough
PE2 9BF
(01733) 890066
info@youngwriters.co.uk

Join in the conversation!

YoungWritersUK   YoungWritersCW   youngwriterscw
youngwriterscw   youngwriterscw-uk